JE7T7

A
HISTORY
OF THE
ISLAMIC PEOPLES

*(Translated from the German of Dr. Weil's Geschichte
der Islamitischen Völker)*

BY

S. KHUDA BUKHSH, M.A., B.C.L.,

Bar-at-Law,
Author of Islamic Civilisation,
*Essays Indian and Islamic, Translator of Von Kremer's Culturgeschichte
des Orients.*

DARF PUBLISHERS LIMITED
LONDON
1985

FIRST PUBLISHED 1914
NEW IMPRESSION 1985

ISBN 1 85077 070 0

Printed and bound in Great Britain
by A. Wheaton & Co. Ltd, Exeter, Devon

INTRODUCTION.

I.

This is neither the place nor the occasion for a review of the great services rendered by Sir Asutosh Mookerjee to the cause of learning in Bengal. Suffice it to say that his eight years' tenure of office as Vice-Chancellor of the Calcutta University is a land-mark which will defy the storm and stress of time. In every sphere of learning his influence will be felt, his services acknowledged; and, as time goes by, his figure will loom larger and larger on the intellectual horizon of his country. The severance of his connection with the University would have been a misfortune at any time; but more than ever is it so at this juncture, when so many things call for his activity and sympathetic guidance.

The Mohamedan Community has special reason to be thankful to him. It was he who introduced Islamic History as a subject of higher study in the University of Calcutta. Hitherto that subject had been neglected, and shockingly so, where it should have attracted special care and interest. Even forsooth in pure centres of Islamic Study Islamic History has been at a discount.

And yet it does not need a very prophetic vision to see its necessity and usefulness. It will teach the Mohamedans what they were, and it will teach the non-Muslims what the Muslims have been in the past. It will set ideals before the one, and it will inspire respect in the other. It will help forward the cause, so dear to us all;—mutual understanding and mutual toleration, the first necessary step to that higher Unity which is at once the dream of the poet, the fervent prayer of the philosopher, the hope of the rising generation, and the true destiny of India.

It is most encouraging, indeed, that this subject should have taken well with students, and we trust it will grow more and more popular as time goes by.

But it is impossible to dismiss this subject without expressing a hope that the authorities will ere long do something to make the study of Islamic History more satisfactory and systematic than it is to-day. Of course we have only just made a beginning ; what possibilities lie beyond ? Who can tell ? Let us, at least, cleave to the sunnier side of doubt.

The present translation owes its origin to the suggestion of Sir Asutosh Mookerjee, and it is therefore only fit and proper that it should stand linked with his great name.

II.

Dr. Gustav Weil is too well-known to require any introduction or recommendation. Among Oriental Scholars in Germany he holds an honoured position, and in spite of continuous researches and the unwearied industry of his countrymen his work still retains the confidence of scholars all over the world. The work of which I now offer an English translation, is a volume at once handy, compact and scholarly—suited most eminently for students who need a safe and trustworthy guide to lead them through the labyrinth of Mohamedan history. It is moreover free from cumbrous foot-notes, which though necessary and useful to scholars, are yet somewhat distressing to students. I have not, however, altogether succeeded in avoiding the foot-notes, but I have been as sparing as possible. I could not overlook the results of more recent investigations and researches, and I have therefore thought it necessary to incorporate them wherever I deemed such a course essential in the interest of learning and scholarship.

Dr. Weil's *Geschichte der Islamitischen Völker* may safely be made the basis of a more detailed and more extended investigation; and as such, I trust, the English translation which I now offer to the Public will be welcome to students and scholars alike, both here and abroad.

I must not, however, omit to mention that I do not at all agree with some of Dr. Weil's observations regarding the Prophet. As I propose to write a separate work dealing with the Prophet and the History of Islam I do not think it wise to burden the pages of this translation with lengthy notes, discussing, criticizing and refuting individual views of the author.

It remains for me now to offer my most grateful thanks to Mr. H. B. Hannah, of the Calcutta Bar, for his uniform kindness and courtesy in revising the proofs of this book; to Dr. Horovitz of Aligarh for his constant and ever ready help in explaining doubtful and difficult passages in the text; and to Miss Effie Whitehead for valuable suggestions, and for unfailing sympathy and encouragement in my work.

CENTRAL LAW COLLEGE, }
Calcutta, 9th April, 1914.

S. K. B.

A
HISTORY
OF THE
ISLAMIC PEOPLES

I

MOHAMED AND THE QUR'AN

1. *Mohamed and the Arabs of his time.*

To understand the Muslims, whose history we have undertaken to write, we must cast a rapid glance at the political and intellectual condition of Arabia, the home of the Prophet Mohamed, the founder of Islam, and also briefly explain how the new faith and the new kingdom arose, and how within a short time they grew into the vast and tremendous power which they eventually became.

In matters religious and political Arabia in the sixth century was the theatre of the wildest confusion. In the south the Jews and the Christians fought for supremacy. Several of the eastern provinces were under the yoke of the Persians; while a portion of the north acknowledged the Byzantine sway.

In Central Arabia alone did the Beduins maintain their ancient freedom ; but, divided as they were into numerous tribes, they not infrequently fought among themselves to the death.

No less unhappy was the condition of their religion. By close contact with Judaism and Christianity many tribes had accepted the Jewish and Christian faiths.

Detached as they were, the inhabitants of Central Arabia alone remained loyal to their old idols. Of these idols—in the shape of men and animals—some were the objects of veneration of this, and some of that tribe. Some tribes, again, worshipped the sun; some the moon; some other heavenly bodies, and some drifted away towards the religion of the magians. Nor were the traces of hero-worship, the cult of tree and stone, entirely absent among the Arabs.

In the life of the Beduins religion, as a rule, filled a very insignificant position, and it was not against a real, genuine attachment to an old time-honoured faith that Islam had to struggle, but against religious indifference, scepticism and gross selfishness.

At the time of Mohamed idol-worship was already nearing its fall. Arab thinkers and Arab poets regarded the idols as worthless, powerless things. Even belief in the world to come was not unknown in Arabia prior to Mohamed, but its widespread diffusion was doubtless due to Islam.

Mekka with its old Temple, the Ka'bah, was the central point of Arabian idolatry. There were lodged the idols of the various tribes, and to it was made the annual pilgrimage. Sacred, indeed, was the season of pilgrimage. Then did strife cease and then did peace reign on earth. Then were life and property held in perfect security. Hence, at the fair and in the markets the barques of commerce rode on a full tide. On the entire population of the Arabian Peninsula the chiefs of the town of Mekka, the holders of the spiritual offices, exercised a profoundly powerful influence, for in their hands lay the fixing of a portion of the sacred months on which depended the security of commerce on the one hand, the outbreak or cessation of hostilities on the other.* Is it any wonder then that the Mekkan aristocracy should keenly combat the new faith—still far removed from success; for the overthrow of the old meant to them total loss of their lucrative rights and privileges?

Mohamed himself belonged to the tribe which constituted the Mekkan aristocracy. His own branch, however, had

---

* [Muir's Life of Mohamed Vol. I, clvi.—Tr.]

become poor, and so great was its proverty that on his birth (April 571 A.D.) his mother Amina could only with difficulty keep a nurse for him. According to some reports his father Abdullah had predeceased him; according to others he died some weeks after.

For several years Mohamed is said to have lived with his nurse among the Beduins. On coming back to his mother he made a journey with her to Medina—her native town. On the return journey she died, and the orphan was taken charge of by his grandfather, Abdul Muttalib, who also died after two years. Mohamed then lived with his uncle Abu Talib, who was too poor to keep him. The young orphan, therefore, was soon compelled to earn his livelihood by tending sheep, an occupation which only the needy and the indigent took to; while the well-to-do inhabitants of Mekka carried on commerce, and for the sale of their wares and products their caravans wandered to Abyssinia, South Arabia, Syria, Egypt and Persia. Mohamed is said to have been to Syria as a camel-driver, but the account, highly coloured as it is, scarcely deserves credit.

But it is on solid historic ground that he appears at the age of five and twenty, in the service of Khadijah, a rich widow, making a commercial journey to South Arabia on her behalf. He married her against the wishes of her father. Thereupon his circumstances improved and his prospects brightened. He was relieved of petty cares and sordid troubles, and could freely devote his dormant powers to matters spiritual. He still continued to carry on commerce for a while, but with little success. Gradually he withdrew from commercial activity, retired more and more into solitude, and in a cave in the neighbourhood of Mekka, he spent at times many weeks together in religious contemplation.

In education Mohamed was very deficient; infact his education was neglected. In his time there was very little

3

culture in Arabia at all. Only poetry stood in full blossom, to the neglect of everything else. Despite his great oratorical gifts Mohamed had very little taste for poetry. The art of writing was very little if at all cultivated, and it is doubtful if Mohamed, in later years, acquired it. His knowledge of Judaism and Christianity was received from oral report—, perhaps from a cousin of his wife who belonged to the group which had renounced idolatry before Islam, but which unsuccessfully sought satisfaction in either of the two religions.

Influenced by him (the cousin of his wife) Mohamed eagerly pondered upon God; upon the life beyond the grave; upon the revelation of divine truth, and strove, with the aid of the religious systems known to him by oral information, to fashion a new religion suited to the Arabs.

The fundamental bases of the new religion were: the subsistence of one God and one only; revelation of God through the Prophet who, though distinguished from other men by prophetic mission, was yet a man of like passion with them; belief in a life to come, where virtue will receive its reward and vice its punishment.

But according to Mohamed the new dispensation was nothing more or less than the one already announced by Ibrahim, whom the Bible and the Arab tradition alike regarded as the progenitor of the Arabs.

He recognised Moses and Christ as great prophets whose teachings were obscured and falsified by their followers. Therefore the laws and ritual of the Old Testament which were unsuited to the Arabs and those dogmas of the new which bordered on polytheism, were to be rejected.

Having arrived at this conclusion Mohamed, with his pious disposition, lively imagination, nervous physical constitution in the quiet, calm of a contemplative life, might easily have led himself into the belief that he was a Prophet inspired by God.

4

Both Eastern and Western research alike point to the fact that Mohamed was subject to epileptic fits, but the superstition of his age regarded him as one possessed of an evil spirit. At first he regarded himself as such, but the belief grew in him that an evil spirit could have no power over a pure soul devoted to God such as his was. The demons, then, were transformed into angels whom he saw alike in dreams and while awake.

To the Supernatural Communion with the angels did he ascribe that unconsciousness which followed continuous, violent mental strain.

During the first years of his prophetic career at least, Mohamed firmly believed in his mission to preach a new religion, or rather to restore the religion of Ibrahim in its original purity. It was this unshaken belief, indeed, which gave him, despite his wavering character and visionary temper, the necessary strength and endurance to bear all the insults and to silently suffer all the injuries which his opponents, for many years, heaped upon him.

In the beginning Mohamed must have been satisfied with delivering his revelation to his nearest relatives and trusted friends. Among the former Abu Bakr fills the first place; among the latter his younger cousin Ali. Both, as Caliphs, later filled a distinguished position in the history of Islam. The great mass of the Mekkans, his uncle not excepted, refused to listen to him. By his anxiety and sympathy for the poor and the weak; by his vigorous invectives against the avarice, the pride, the superciliousness of the Mekkan aristocracy, he gradually won a number of converts from men in humbler stations in life. The distinguished Mekkans who tolerated him at first gradually perceived the danger which threatened them. No longer content, therefore, with merely ridiculing or despising him as a sooth-sayer or a sorcerer, they set him down as a liar, and persecuted him as a corrupter of religion. Mohamed and his influential converts, assured of protection from their family, persisted in the new religion—for the honour of the tribe was of greater moment than faith in the idols—though protection only extended to cases of gross ill-treatment. Slaves, freedmen and others who were without protection, were reduced to the necessity of either renouncing their new faith or abandoning their old home.

Abyssinia was the country fixed for emigration. There, under Christian rule, they could expect the best protection against idol worship.

Mohamed, however, continued his attack against idolatry and the denial of a future life, and sought to effect his purpose by vivid, thrilling, telling descriptions of the terrors of hell and the joys of paradise.

He further threatened the irreligious town with its approaching doom, and related how God had destroyed the older ones and their inhabitants for their sins and their disbelief. When he referred to the history of the earlier prophets the Arabs demanded miracles of him such as had been worked by the prophets of yore. To this Mohamed could offer no other answer than this, that the greatest miracle was his revelation, and that God, in his mercy, left open to them this one pretext, because He knew that, like the hardened sinners before, they would not believe.

Then followed for Mohamed a period of deep dejection and profound despair. The darkness thickened and the shadows of despair began to gather around him. He went indeed to the extent of making a compromise with his persecutors. He acknowledged their idols as intermediaries between man and Allah. But he soon perceived his error. He took courage; he recalled the concession; and he declared it to have been the suggestion of Satan.

Owing to his constant asperity the number of his opponents increased day by day, and their attitude became more and more insulting and hostile. His power, however, about this time received a sudden accession of strength by two conversions which were an ample set off for much apostacy. The one was that of Hamza, called, for his courage, the lion of God; and the other was that of Omar, later on the second Caliph, the stoutest support of Islam, and the most splendid character among the companions of the Prophet.

In Hamza (an uncle of Mohamed) was awakened the feelings of compassion and family honour. He acknowledged Islam in order that he might be able all the more effectively to appear as the protector of his deeply injured nephew.

Omar passed for one of the most violent opponents of Mohamed, and is even said to have designed to kill him when he suddenly found that his own sister and her husband had accepted the teachings of the Prophet. He rushed into their house and assaulted them. But he soon repented of his rashness, read the piece of the Qur'an which he found with them, and was, as Muslims assert, so impressed by its noble diction and lofty contents, that he forthwith repaired to Mohamed, acknowledged him as the Prophet of God, and even compelled him, under his own and Hamza's protection, to visit the Temple which he had no longer ventured to enter. These conversions and their consequences tended only further to embitter his opponents against him. It was not long before they mutually pledged themselves to put Mohamed and his family under a ban.

Thus outlawed, they retired to a ravine in the chief valley, and lived there in dire affliction, as they could obtain provisions only from a great distance or through friends secretly. For two years, at the very least, did this state of affairs last, and not without difficulty did the friends of Mohamed succeed in getting the ban removed. His supporters at this time were not very numerous, and probably Mohamed did not then appear to be very dangerous to his opponents. The least effort on their part would have crushed him. His position in his native town could not have been very cheerful, for shortly after he left for Taif in the hopes of finding among its inhabitants a friendly reception and a willing ear for Islam.

Taif lies east of Mekka.* In his expectations he was deceived, and deceived grievously. On his return to Mekka he felt all the more sad and depressed, for both Khadijah who was unfailing in her encouragement, and his uncle Abu Talib, who was heroic in his support, were shortly torn away from him by the all-destroying hand of death.

Things looked bleak and dreary. Not until the 11th year of his mission and fifty-first of his life did affairs take a happy turn for him and his religion, by the conversion of some pilgrims from Yathrib, the town later on chosen by Mohamed for his residence and subsequently called Medina. The converts spread the new teachings in their native town. In the following year they came to the annual fair in larger numbers. In the third year, when Islam had made still greater progress among them, they invited Mohamed to come over to them and swore protection to him. The speedy attachment of the Medinites to Mohamed is to be explained, firstly, by the fact that his mother came from Medina and her people considered the duty of protecting him as a point of honour ; then, by close contact with Jewish tribes settled among them, and who expected their Messiah, the Medinites were long prepared for a new prophet. Finally, the town of Medina, jealous of the importance of Mekka, looked eagerly forward to position and distinction through Mohamed and his religion. Mohamed sent his followers on in advance to Medina. Some months after, he along with Abu Bakr fled

* [Muir's Life of Mohamed. Vol, II, pp. 207.]

secretly from Mekka. He probably feared detention or ill-treatment on the way.

With this emigration, called the Hegira in Arabic, begins the Mohamedan era. Although the real emigration took place in September 622 A. D., the Mohamedan era dates from the 16th of July—the first day of the then Arab year.

On his arrival in Medina Mohamed's first care was to provide a new home for the emigrants who had come with him and before him. He, on that account, established a brotherhood involving, even to the exclusion of blood relations, the right of mutual inheritance. He soon settled the rules of worship, and built a mosque, in which was performed a short prayer five times a day. Mohamed, in the first period of his residence at Medina, tried, by all manner of concessions, to win over the Jews settled there.

For instance he fixed the Kiblah towards Jerusalem (the side to which one turned his face at prayer). He appointed the 10th day of the first month as a day of fast, and gave permission to the converts to observe the sabbath. But when he failed in his hopes, for the Jews expected a Messiah of the family of David, he became their bitterest enemy. Later he fixed the Kiblah towards Mekka, appointed the month of Ramadhan as the month of fast, and Friday as the day of rest. The most important measure of Mohamed, in the first year of the emigration, was the sanction which he gave in the name of God to war against the infidel. Finally he enjoined it as a religious duty. Fighting the enemy became the most splendid of virtues. To those slain in battle he promised the joys of paradise, to those who shirked or evaded it he, by divine decree, threatened an ignominious death.

The first campaigns of Mohamed when he could scarcely put 100 men in the field, were really no more than predatory expeditions, directed against the Mekkan caravans which, in their commercial journeys, passed through the neighbourhood of Medina. The paucity of numbers was due to the fact that the majority of the Medinites were still unconverted, and, though pledged to protect Mohamed, were under no obligation to join him in offensive warfares.

The Mekkans, indeed, were careful enough. They either sent their caravans with a strong escort, or took a circuitous route to Syria. To take them by surprise, he organised a predatory expedition during one of the holy months in which Arabs enjoyed perfect peace. The circumstances of these expeditions are very significant of the character of Mohamed and his revelations at this period. We notice, here, as we do in his acceptance of the Pre-Islamic belief in the intermediary character of the idols, a certain want of definite principle and the beginning of a series of acts, committed or approved, for the sole purpose of chastising the heathens and intercepting their commerce—acts which without reference to a severe ethical code, must be disapproved and condemned.

Mohamed sent for his brother-in-law Abdullah, handed over to him a piece of writing, under seal, and directed him to set out for South Arabia with twelve companions to carry out the orders contained in the sealed cover. He further directed him to abstain from reading the contents until the 3rd day of his departure. Abdullah obeyed. On the third day he broke open the seal, and found only the following words : Proceed with thy companions to the valley of Nakhlah (south east of Arabia) and lie in wait for the Mekkan caravan. Abdullah naturally interpreted these words to mean that he was to attack the caravan. He did so and successfully.

Two men were taken captive. One was slain. Abdullah brought the whole cargo as booty to Medina. To put an end to all discussion with Abdullah on the subject of predatory expeditions, undertaken in a holy month, Mohamed brought forth a revelation.

To throw off responsibility from his shoulders he had given an ambiguous message. But when the Muslims of Medina waxed indignant and blamed him for the desecration of the holy month, he disavowed the action of Abdullah and contended that he had overstepped his instructions, and that he had never, as a matter of fact, ordered him to attack the caravan in the holy month.

When he saw, however, that he was nevertheless regarded as the author of that wanton wrong, he withdrew from the Mekkans the security enjoyed by them for purposes of commerce in the four holy months. The Qur'anic verses were revealed in which war against the infidel was declared lawful at all times, because to their many sins they had added one other, and that was the sin of expelling the Prophet from his home.

We could not have acquitted Mohamed of blood-guiltiness on the occasion of the attack on this caravan even if his biographers had not reported many other assassinations recommended ; nay, even regarded as meritorious by him—assassinations of women, not excepted.

Even before his flight to Medina Mohamed had fallen from the path of truth and rectitude.

To cite only one instance—he related the whole history of the prophets of the Old and New Testaments embellished by many Judaic and Christian fables and legend, and asserted that the angel Gabriel had revealed them to him.

This the Mekkans discredited and, not without reason, ascribed his knowledge of matters scriptural to his intercourse with foreigners versed in the scriptures.

The first encounter between the Mekkans and the Mohamedans took place in the second year of the Hegira at Badr, a station well-supplied with water, between Mekka and Medina. With an army of over three hundred men Mohamed had started to attack and to plunder the rich Mekkan caravan on its way home from Syria.

Abu Sufyan, the leader of the caravan, got wind of the design. He sent a messenger to Mekka summoning his compatriots to the defence of their property. Before the arrival of the summoned aid, some 900 strong, Abu Sufyan, who knew that Mohamed was lying in wait at Badr, managed to avoid that place by taking the route along the sea coast. As soon as the news of the safety of the caravan reached the Mekkan camp, a portion of the men who had only taken up arms out of fear of losing their property, showed a desire to return home. Others—bitter enemies of the Prophet—and men fond of war, resolved to proceed to Badr. This decision was adopted— though many persisted in their refusal and returned home. In the camp of the Prophet a similiar indecision prevailed. There was the prospect of the booty, but it was not a very bright one in a battle against overwhelming odds. But no less powerful was the consideration that if they failed to deal a blow in the interest of the new faith they would be branded as cowards.

Thus they came to a bloody encounter in which the Medinites, trained in war and contemptuous of death, won a victory over the effeminate Mekkan traders and carried off a rich booty. Mohamed himself remained far away from the actual fight. In a hut he unceasingly prayed until he sank exhausted. On regaining consciousness he announced victory to his men through the help of heavenly troops. This first military success led to the rapid growth of Islam. To the poor community, arms, horses and camels captured in war, as also a fair sum of money received in exchange for captives, meant an accession of fresh strength. This military triumph increased their confidence, multiplied their numbers, and cheered them on to a path of further glory. The first victim of the victorious troops was the Jewish tribe of Kainuka. It was compelled to surrender, and would probably have been completely annihilated, had not Abdullah, the Son of Ubai, the chief of the Khazrajites, assisted them in their retreat.* Their belongings, however, fell entirely into the hands of the Muslims. About this time, too, took place the murders of several men, dangerous or odious to Islam.

Thus a reign of terror was established by men on the side of the Prophet. The result was that all individual opposition was crushed, and the weak sought safety in the bosom of Islam. The Mekkans, in the meantime, were not idle or inactive. Their interest as well as their honour called for vengeance for the defeat at Badr. To reconnoitre and to make alliance with men hostile to Mohamed, Abu Sufyan before the end of the second year of the Hegira, had already made an excursion right up to the neighbourhood of Medina. In the following year (625 A. D.) he set out at the head of some 3000 men for Medina, and pitched his camp to the east of the town. Informed by friendly Arabs, of the movements of the Mekkans, Mohamed decided to confine himself to the defence of the town. But his fanatical followers declaring this as a piece of cowardice, he was compelled to march out with some 2000 men. Of these well-nigh a third, under the leadership of Abdullah, mentioned already, who hated in his heart both Mohamed and Islam, returned to Medina. At Ohod, north of Medina, the Muslims, in spite of their small number, successfully beat the Mekkans, until the archers, who were to repel the cavalry of the enemy, forsook the place assigned to them. The brave Khalid, leading the Mekkan cavalry, thus found an opportunity of attacking the enemy from the rear. A dreadful panic took possession of the faithful and they took to flight. Mohamed himself was wounded and he fainted away. The report that he was dead caused still

---

* The Khazrajites were an Arab tribe settled in Medina. The tribe of Kainuka were the allies of the Khazrajites.

further havoc among his troops. A trusted follower, recognizing him by his eye—for he was covered with a coat of mail, a helmet, a visor—brought him to a place of safety.

The Mekkans, in the meanwhile, believing the rumour of his death, did not worry themselves any further. Satisfied with their achievement they wended their way homeward. Only when the battle had ended and probably a portion of the army was already on its homeward march did Abu Sufyan learn that Mohamed was still alive. He decided, in the following year, to attack him afresh.

To show that he was in no way dis-spirited Mohamed pursued the enemy, for some miles, the day after the battle, in which he lost seventy men, his uncle among them, whose corpse, along with those of the others, was horribly mutilated.

To the defeat at Ohod, which lowered the reputation of Mohamed to the same extent as the victory at Badr had raised it, we might add some other failures, but they were insignificant raids which need not detain us.

For the loss suffered at Ohod the only set-off that Mohamed could offer to his followers was the expulsion of the Jews of the tribe of Nadir in the 4th year of the Hegira. The Jews capitulated and emigrated. Mohamed declared their property his, since it was not acquired in war, and divided it among the poor Mekkan refugees. Towards the end of the year (4th year of the Hegira) he again advanced to Badr with a fairly strong army, to show that he utterly disregarded the threat of leading a fresh attack against him held out by Abu Sufyan after the battle of Ohod. The Mekkans were not prepared and had indeed no intention of fighting.

Towards the end of the 5th year (beginning of 627 A. D.), the Mekkans started for Medina a second time, under the leadership of Abu Sufyan. They were 10,000 strong—the

14

Mekkans and their allies of the Beduin tribes. The Medinites were depressed. They could scarcely put 3,000 men in the field, and they further apprehended an attack from the Jewish tribe of Kuraizah. This time Mohamed decided not to meet the enemy in the open field, but only to defend the town. As soon as he was informed of the approach of the hostile army, upon the advice of a Persian, he caused a ditch to be dug. Inexperienced though the Arabs were in the art of laying a siege—this defensive method (however imperfect) was in fact enough to prevent a wholesale attack. But the Mekkans were further hampered by a tempest that broke out and the dissension that arose among their allies. The result was a retreat. They returned home disappointed and unsuccessful.

Though the siege of Medina inflicted but little material loss—still it affected, as did the battle at Ohod, the reputation of Mohamed as a warrior and a Prophet, because contrary to all the established and cherished traditions of the Arabs, instead of giving battle to the enemy, he took shelter behind the wall and the rampart.

Once again did Mohamed direct his attention towards the Jews who had been meddling with the Mekkans, and he compelled them to surrender.

The Jews, the Banu Kuraizah, already mentioned, had been the allies of the Ausites (the second great Arab tribe settled in Medina), and had hoped to secure, through their intervention, as favourable terms as did the Banu Kainuka through the intervention of Abdullah. But unfortunately the chief of the Ausites had been wounded during the siege of Medina, and when Mohamed summoned him to act as an arbitrator he condemned men* to death and women and children to slavery. This expedition was followed by several others against the hostile Beduin tribes. These gradually and insensibly effaced

---

* Some six to nine hundred men.

15

the unfavourable impression created by the siege of Medina, and towards the end of the 6th year of the Hegira Mohamed resolved, with his friends and allies, to make a pilgrimage to Mekka. Having announced his intention solemnly and in the name of God, he had no alternative but to undertake the pilgrimage. He had a small following. The Arab account fixes it between 7 to 1400 men. But what he relied on most was the reluctance of the Arabs to shed blood in a holy month—although he himself did not hesitate to do so. He stopped on the frontier of the holy territory when he found the Mekkans firm in refusing him admission to the town. After long negotiations they at last agreed that he was to go back that year, but the following year he was to be permitted three days' stay in Mekka for the purpose of pilgrimage.

Painful, indeed, it was to the Prophet and his companions to be so near the holy town, and yet to go without the pilgrimage. This peace was big with great results—though at first sight it seemed disadvantageous to the Prophet. By this treaty Mohamed was indirectly acknowledged as the equal of the proud Mekkan aristocracy; for this treaty placed him, in a certain measure, on terms of equality with them. The right of admission into Mekka the following year was a victory which considerably heightened his reputation among the Arabs. He could now send his missionaries to all parts of Arabia, make proselytes, and form alliances. To materially strengthen his power, to enrich his supporters and thereby multiply their number, to remove any damaging impression which his unsuccessful attempt at pilgrimage might have created—he marched against the Jews of Khaibar who, at a distance of 4 to 5 days' journey, north-east of Medina, had their goods and effect. Their forts were successively stormed and plundered, and unable to hold out they at last surrendered.

They resigned their property in favour of the victors, but were permitted to remain as their tenants on condition that

16

they should make over to them half of the annual produce. Similar terms were granted to other Jews in the neighbourhood of Khaibar. Thus did Mohamed secure means, more and more, to increase and strengthen his soldiery.

Between 628 and 629 A.D. several other campaigns were undertaken against the Beduins. The number of the faithful steadily grew, and the idea became fixed in Mohamed's mind that Islam, as the only true religion, was a religion meant not only for the Arabs but for all mankind. Even before the conquest of Mekka he had sent messengers to the neighbouring princes of Persia, Byzantium, Abyssinia. He also invited the Christian governor of Egypt and several Arab chiefs under Persian and Byzantine sway to accept his religion. These messengers received more or less a hostile reception. Only the Greek governor treated them in a friendly spirit and sent valuable presents to the Prophet—though he did not accept Islam. Among the presents were two slave girls. One of these, Mary, fascinated the Prophet so completely that, for her sake, he neglected the rest of his wives. After the death of his first wife, Mohamed married some dozen wives; some out of love, some for reasons of State.

Of these were Maimuna, aunt of the intrepid Khalid who shortly after with Amr lbn Aass was converted to Islam; Ayesha, the daughter of Abu Bakr; Hafza, the daughter of Omar and Zainab, the sister of Abdullah, notorious for his violation of the sanctity of the holy month. The Qur'an limits the number of legitimate wives to four, but Mohamed was to be an exception to the rule. In matters sexual public opinion was lax in Arabia. There was unbounded polygamy, and thus the wives of the Prophet had to submit to their lot. But when, in the person of Mary, an Abyssinian slave, they found a dangerous rival, they could endure it no longer, and Mohamed, to appease them, made a solemn promise to keep himself hence forward away and apart from her.

17

3

He spent a whole month in a garret without visiting his wives. Then followed some verses of the Qur'an whereby Allah released Mohamed from his promise regarding Mary, and threatened his wives, should they persist in their obstinacy, to give him, in their place, partners—better and more obedient, than they.

Mohamed's *Harem* occupies a considerable place in the Qur'an. He married Ayesha when she was scarcely fifteen. She had accompanied him in one of his campaigns. On the return journey she was left behind and arrived in Medina with the captain of the rear-guard some hours later. The whole of Medina talked of this incident, and in the presence of friends even Mohamed made no secret of his doubts as to her fidelity— for her explanation as to the delay was anything but satisfactory. After the lapse of a month his love for her or rather his regard for her father (his old and trusted friend) prevailed over his sentiments of jealousy and revenge, and, after a severe epileptic fit, he in the name of God, proclaimed her innocent.

One other revelation relating to Mohamed's wedded life deserves a passing reference here. It shows how easily the Prophet, in matters sexual, was carried away by his passions.

Zainab, the wife of Zaid* attracted his attention. Zaid, not failing to notice the attention of the Prophet, divorced her— whereupon Mohamed married her. This marriage was regarded as objectionable for two reasons. Not only was it deemed ungenerous of Mohamed to have accepted such a sacrifice from Zaid, one of his first and devoted followers; but it was also contrary to the general practice which condemned marriage with the wife of an adopted son who was regarded in the light of a natural son and whose wife after divorce the father could not marry.

To put an end to all adverse comment he declared the hitherto obtaining practice of adoption as foolish, and its practice

---

* A quondam slave and then the adopted son of the Prophet.

in future as sinful. To foster the growth of the belief that Zaid had divorced his wife, contrary to his wishes, he put forward a verse of the Qur'an in which God was made to say how he (Mohamed), in spite of his love for her, exhorted Zaid to remain loyal to her, and how, even after the divorce, out of fear of men he hesitated to marry her, until so enjoined by God. And then, in sooth, he did so, firstly, to show that the idle talk of man was of no consequence where the question was one of the will of God, and secondly, by his own example to invest the law relating to adoption with greater weight.

On the occasion of this marriage one other verse of the Qur'an was revealed which shut off the wives of the Prophet from the rest of the world, and also imposed certain restrictions upon the dress and demeanour of all believing women. *

Thus, by his jealousy, (extending even beyond the grave, for he forbad his wives' remarriage after his death) women were excluded, once and for all, from public life, and even in domestic circles their society was confined only to women and nearest relatives.

The Muslim wife was thus reduced to slavery, while among the heathen Arabs, she was the partner and companion of her husband. She was now to take part only in her husband's domestic joys; while, before, she enlivened his social and public life. She was, among the Beduins, as among the Western knights of the middle ages, an object of worship and veneration, Islam converted her into an object of compassion and distrust. True, she was called his *Harim* (a sacred thing), but by this they understood one whom not her own virtues but only the veil and the bolt and the eunuch could save from fall. †

* [See, Muir's Life of Mohamed, Vol. III. pp. 231 et seq.—Tr.]

† [See, Sir Charles Lyall's Introduction to Ancient Arabian poetry. Tr.]

Just as the letter of Mohamed to the Governor of Egypt, inviting him to the faith of Islam, had a fateful result on the position of women in Islamic society—so might we ascribe the genesis of several mischievous laws to the embassy which Mohamed sent to a Christian chief of the Arabs on the Syrian borders.

The former was the cause of the intervention of God in Mohamed's domestic affairs, resulting in the assertion of man's superiority over woman—the latter was the source of several mischievous laws, regarded as sacred to the present day.

The chief ordered the execution of one of Mohamed's messengers. This execution led to the first war between the Byzantines and the Muslims which ended disastrously for the Muslims at Muta (629 A. D.) in the neighbourhood of the Dead Sea. Three generals fell (one after another), and with difficulty did Khalid succeed in saving the remnant of the troops. A second expedition against the Byzantines in the following year yielded but small result. It received scant assistance from the allies of the Prophet. Mohamed, therefore, caused the ninth chapter of the Qur'an to be proclaimed, which contains quite a new law of war and a new law of nations.

Henceforth none but Muslims could enter the holy territory and its neighbourhood, but beyond it idol-worship was to be destroyed, root and branch. Jews and Christians could only be tolerated on submission and on payment of the tribute.

The language of the Qur'an was interpreted to mean that a duty was cast on the faithful to fight non-Muslims until conversion or subjection, and continually to oppress the subject races even if they were other than idol-worshippers.

The Caliph Omar made various exceptions to the law requiring the humiliation of non-Muslims, but his successors sharpened and extended the law in proportion to their religious fanaticism.

The ordinance, which under Sultan Nasir, appeared in Egypt in the XIVth century, shows best the terrible consequences which flowed from the language of the Qur'an.

The Christians, to be distinguished at first sight from the faithful, should henceforth, it says, wear a blue turban, and for a similar reason the Jews a yellow one. Jewish and Christian women, likewise, should carry the distinguishing badge on their breast. The unfaithful are forbidden to carry arms or to ride horses, and even on mules they are to sit sideways and use a simple, unadorned saddle. They are to move out of the way of the Muslims and yield the middle of the street to them. In large gatherings they are to get up* in presence of Muslims and are not to raise their voices above theirs. Their houses are not to be higher than those of the Muslims. They are not publicly to celebrate Palm Sunday nor are they to ring bells or to make proselytes. It is forbidden to them to keep Muslims as slaves, or to purchase captives of war, or what otherwise would have fallen as booty to the Muslims. Jews and Christians visiting public baths, are to make themselves known by the use of a small bell round their neck. They are not to use Arabic inscriptions on their signets nor are they to teach the Qur'an to their children. They are not to put Muslims to hard work, and on pain of death they are forbidden to have intercourse with Muslim women. No Jew or Christian is to be employed in the State chanceries, a prohibition dating from the time of the Caliph Omar, and honoured more in the breach than in its observance.

The ignorance of the first Arabs and Turks in matters of government, and their subsequent indifference thereto and their scant business-like capacity, made the services of the Christians and the Jews indispensable to them in the work of administration.

---

* To get up, *i.e.*, to show respect to them.

After the conquest of Mekka, which took place in the Ramadhan of the 8th year of the Hegira, the new laws of war were promulgated and the second expedition against the Byzantines undertaken.*

Some Mekkans by taking part in a night attack on the Khuzaites, the allies of Mohamed, violated the peace which extended not only to the Muslims and the Mekkans but also to their respective allies. This incident was most opportune for Mohamed who had his eyes fixed upon Mekka, and who now felt sufficiently strong to conquer the holy town. He accordingly decided to avenge this violation of the peace, although Abu Sufyan himself came to Medina to offer apology and seek pardon on behalf of the entire community.

Abu Sufyan was dismissed with a non-committing answer. But the preparations for war were conducted with such zeal and secrecy that even before the announcement of a formal declaration Mohamed with ten thousand men had pitched his camp in the neighbourhood of Mekka. The town could offer no resistance, and thus no alternative was left to the chiefs but to surrender and to acknowledge Mohamed not only as their temporal ruler but also as a Prophet of God. Mohamed was satisfied with the result, and prohibited bloodshed where no opposition was offered. Only at one of the gates of the town a small body of fanatics were repelled by the sword. A general amnesty was proclaimed—only some fifteen men were excluded from it. Of these several were pardoned at the intercession of Mohamed's friends, and several took safety in flight. Only four persons were executed.

When order was restored in the town Mohamed repaired to the temple, performed the circuit round it according to the old heathen customs, and cleansed it of the idols there.

---

* This expedition resulted in the battle of Tabuk.

Then, on one of the hills of the town he received the oath of allegiance, as also the vow to follow him in all wars against the infidels. At the same time he again declared Mekka a holy town in which only by way of exception did God permit him to shed blood but which henceforward was to remain inviolable. He pacified the Medinites who feared that he might make Mekka, his birth place, the seat of his future residence.

During his stay at Mekka several generals were sent to the neighbouring tribes to reduce them to submission, to destroy idols and to demolish heathen places of worship.

He himself advanced at the head of 12,000 men against the Hawazin tribes and the inhabitants of Taif, who under the leadership of Malik Ibn Auf had taken up their post between Mekka and Taif.

When the Muslims came to the valley of Honain they were suddenly attacked by a Beduin ambuscade. A panic took possession of the Mohamedans which was deliberately increased by many Arabs who were hardly genuine converts, and thus the troops took to a wild flight. Abbas the uncle of the Prophet brought the flying army to a place of safety ; then they fought afresh until the enemy fled, leaving a rich booty and numerous captives to the victors. After this the town of Taif was besieged, where a portion of the defeated army had taken refuge, but the Muslims were as powerless against it as formerly the Mekkans had been against the entrenchment at Medina. After a siege of several weeks Mohamed had to leave without effecting his purpose. After the lapse of a year the town voluntarily surrendered. According to some reports Mohamed was willing to grant many concessions to them, such as freedom from the poor tax, immunity from participating in the holy war and permission to retain for a year their idol Al Lat. When the treaty however was being drawn up Omar stepped forward and

23

prevailed upon Mohamed to accept nothing but unconditional submission.

The submission of Taif was a herald for the submission of the inhabitants of the valleys.

From the most outlying provinces came messengers bringing homage to the victorious Prophet. After the conquest of Mekka and the announcement of the new laws of war, no other choice lay to the Arabs except the choice between the Qur'an and the sword.

It did not press heavily on the Beduins, indifferent as they were to matters of faith, to confess belief in one God, in Mohamed as the Prophet of God, and in the Day of Judgment.

Nothing more was required of the converts than ablution and prayer, a fixed poor tax, pilgrimage once in life to Mekka. Of the prohibitions the most important was not murder, theft, adultery and similar offences common alike to all religious societies; but the seeking of tribal aid in disputes, as had been the case hitherto, instead of the help of law and constituted authority. Nor was this unreasonable, for without it no fusion of the tribes into one compact whole was possible, nor any ordered government practicable.

Mohamed was now the *de facto* master of the whole of Arabia. Even the unfaithful (numerous as they were, and as their rapid apostacy after his death shows) found themselves constrained to acknowledge him as the Prophet of God, with their tongue if not with their heart. The next pilgrimage (632 A. D.) was suffered to be celebrated by none save Muslims at Mekka, cleansed of idols. In their midst did Mohamed repair to teach and instruct them in the various laws of Islam. In one of the discourses that he delivered he introduced the pure lunar year for all times, and laid down rules and regulations regarding the pilgrimage—rules and regulations calculated to inspire in the

24

pilgrim sentiments of worship and devotion. They were these :—
he had to cover himself with a single piece of cloth ; he was to
avoid all quarrels and disputes ; he was not to go about hunting ;
he was to renounce all sensual pleasures ; he was to visit first the
temple in Mekka and then the other holy places in the neighbourhood. Finally he was to slay the animal which he had
brought with him for sacrifice. It was to be used partly for his
own and partly for the benefit of his people and partly for the
purposes of charity. *

As regards the poor, Mohamed emphasised the duties which
the rich and the powerful owed to them. Even the helpless
wife he recommended to the compassion of her husband, and
secured for her a share in his property. Finally, he forbade
games of chance, use of animals not properly slain, the blood
and flesh of swine ; but, indispensable as was camel's flesh to the
Arabs, he did not think it fit to import into Islam further dietary
restrictions drawn from Judaism.

A few months after his return from this pilgrimage Mohamed
made preparations for a third expedition against the Byzantines,
but this did not set out till after his death. After a fortnight's
fever he died on the 8th of June 632 A.D. at the age of 63
according to the lunar and 61 according to the solar year.

Mohamed's biographers ascribe his death to a poisoned piece
of mutton which the sister of a slain Jew is said to have given
him on the occasion of the Khaibar expedition. This campaign
took place four years before his death, and even if the fact of the
attempted poison was proved, the connexion between the two
can scarcely be established.

As happened later in the case of the Caliph Abu Bakr, very
probably such a fable was invented—(for they could not make

---

* [See, Khuda Bukhsh, Islamic Civilisation pp. 47 et seq ; see also the
Second Chapter of Von Kremer's Culturgeschichte des Orients. An English
translation is now in course of publication. Tr.]

4

him ascend into heaven like Christ) to glorify him with the death of a martyr. * And what indeed was not invented in the first century of the Hegira to glorify the Prophet? He was created before every other thing in the world. On his birth a shining light appeared in the east; the fire of Magians went out; a violent earthquake shook the throne of the Khosroes. He was born calling out: "There is no God but God and I am the Prophet of God." Trees protected him and flowers greeted him as he passed through the desert, and even rocks saluted him as the Prophet of God. Such a one marked out in such a way could not die of ordinary fever. He should at least die a martyr's death. The personal contributions of Mohamed to these legends it is difficult to assess. One of the oldest authorities report him as having said in his last illness that he felt as if the veins of his heart were bursting in consequence of the morsel that he took at Khaibar, and the informant adds that Muslims might infer from this that God made Mohamed die as a martyr after he had glorified him by the seal of prophetship.

However that may be, there is no doubt that he had frequent recourse to all sorts of fraud and imposture to secure his purpose; calling into his service the angel Gabriel to reveal things which he could not himself believe.

But we must not on this account condemn him as a mere fraud, for unless he wished to undo his whole work nothing else was left to him but to act the part to the end, for which he had originally believed himself to be marked out by God. †

---

* Among the Muslims every one was a martyr whose death was connected in any way with a holy war.

† [See, Freeman's History and Conquest of the Saracens pp. 46-47. Of the European writers the most appreciative in English, of recent times, is Bosworth Smith's Mohamed and Mohamedanism, and in German Krehl's Das Leben des Muhammed. Of course I have not forgotten Higgins and Davenport, but they can scarcely lay a claim to scholarship. Tr.]

Justly indeed might he claim to be the benefactor of his country. It was he who united into one nation the scattered tribes, locked in perpetual strife, and bound them together by the ties of faith in one God and the immortality of the soul. It was he who purified Arabia of idolatry and released it from foreign bondage. It was he who substituted an inviolable and inviolate system of law (imperfect it might be) in the place of blood-revenge, law of might and wild caprice. It was he who laid down the law for all times. It was he who softened the hard lot of the slave, and showed a paternal care for the poor, the orphan and the widow. It was he who assigned a share to them in the poor-tax and in the booty.

The Qur'an condemns cruelty, pride, arrogance, extravagance, calumny, games of chance, the use of intoxicants, and other vices which debase men and destroy social life. It recommends faith in God and resignation to his will. This was meant, as will appear in the sequel, as subversive neither of human activity nor of moral freedom. But in consequence of some passages of the Qur'an the doctrine of divine decree has been misunderstood here and there.

Mohamed set a shining example to his people. Apart from his weakness for the fair sex, his character was pure and stainless. His house, his dress, his food—they were characterised by a rare simplicity. So unpretentious was he that he would receive from his companions no special mark of reverence, nor would he accept any service from his slave which he could do himself. Often and often indeed was he seen in the market purchasing provisions; often and often was he seen mending his clothes in his room, or milking a goat in his courtyard. He was accessible to all, and at all times. He visited the sick and was full of sympathy for all, and whenever politics was not in the way he was generous and forbearing to a degree. Unlimited was his benevolence and generosity, and so was his anxious care for the welfare of the community. Despite innumerable presents which from all quarters unceasingly poured in for him; despite rich booty which streamed in—he left very little behind, and even that he regarded as State property. Afer his death his property passed to the State and not to Fatima, his only daughter, the wife of Ali.

Besides Fatima Mohamed had other children, but tradition, is discrepant as to their number. But this much is certain that all save Fatima predeceased him. Of his issue we will only mention Ruqqaya and Umm Kulthum whom the Caliph Othman married—one after another—both children of his first wife Khadija, and Ibrahim (son of the Coptic slave, Mary) whose premature death the Prophet deeply mourned. He did not weep aloud " for fear of annoying the Lord, and because of his belief that he would get him back." One of his companions finding him bathed in tears, asked him whether he had not forbidden lamentation for the dead. He replied ' I have condemned weeping aloud, scratching of the face and tearing of one's clothes. Shedding of tears, said he, on the occasion of a misfortune is a sign of compassion—shouting and shrieking is the work of devil.'

Though in no way free from the prejudices and superstitions of the time, he said to people who were disposed to regard the eclipse of the sun on the day of Ibrahim's death as a sign and a token of grief, that sun and moon care not for the life or death of a mere mortal.

[*Bibliography.*

1. Lives of Mohamed and history of the early days of Islam :—

Ibn Ishaq, ob. about 150 A. H, **767** A.D.: his work (so far as is at present known) exists in two abridgements only : that by Ibn Hisham, ob. 218 A. H., 833 A.D, which has been published by Wüstenfeld, Göttingen, 1860, and later by Zubair Pasha ; and that by Tabari, ob. 310 A.H., 922 A.D., embodied in his *Chronicle*, published at Leyden, 1882-1885.

Waqidi, ob. 207 A. H., 823 A. D., author of a treatise on Mohamed's Campaigns, of which an imperfect edition was issued by Von Kremer, Calcutta, 1856; an abridged translation of a far more perfect copy was made by Wellhausen and published with the title *Muhammed in Medina*, Berlin, 1882.

Ibn Sa'd, Secretary of Waqidi, ob. 230 A. H., 845 A. D.; author of an encyclopœdic work on the Prophet, his Followers, etc., published at Berlin under the superintendence of Sachau.

Yaqubi, ob. about 292 A. H. 905 A.D., author of a history in two parts, Pre-Islamic and Islamic, published by Houtsma, Leyden, 1883.

Ibn-al-Athir, ob. 630 A. H., 1233 A. D:, author of a universal history, published at Leyden and in Egypt.

Diyarbekri, ob. 982 A, H., 1574 A.D., author of a life of the Prophet, followed by a sketch of Islamic history, called Tarikh Al-Khamis, published at Cairo, 1302 A. H.

Halabi, ob. 1044 A. H., 1634 A. D., author of a Life of the Prophet, called Insan al-uyun, published at Cairo, 1292.

2. Books of Tradition (*i. e.* collections of sayings attributed to the Prophet, and traced back to him through a series of trustworthy witnesses) :—

Musnad of Ibn Hanbal.

Collection by Bukhari, ob. 256 A.H, 870. A.D.

Collection by Muslim, ob. 261 A. H., 875 A.D.

Collection by Tirmidhi, ob. 279 A. H., 892 A.D.

Collection by Nasa'i, ob. 303 A. H., 916 A.D.

Other authentic collections are by Malik Ibn Anas, ob. 179 A. H., 795 A.D.; by Ibn Majah, ob. 273 A. H., 887 A.D., and Abu Dawud, ob. 275 A. H., 889 A.D.

3. History of Mekka and Medina :—

History of Mekka by Azraqi, ob. about 245 A. H., 859 A.D., edited by Wüstenfeld, Leipzig, 1858.

History of Medina by Samhudi, ob. 911 A. H., 1505 A.D., published at Cairo, 1255 A. H : epitomised by Wüstenfeld in his *Geschichte der Stadt Medina*, Göttingen, 1873.

Modern works on Mekka and Medina.

Burckhardt's Travels.

Burton's Pilgrimage to Al-medinah and Meccah.

A. H. Keane, Six months in the Hejaz.

Soubhy, Pélerinage à la Mecque et à Médine, Cairo, 1894.

Muhammad Basha Sadik, The Pilgrim's Guide (Arabic), Cairo 1313 A.H., 1895 A.D.

Gervais—Courtellemont, Mon voyage à la Mecque, Paris, 1897.

4. Goldziher, Muhammadanische Studien, Halle, 1889, 1890.

and Abhandlungen zur Arabischen Litteratur, Leyden 1896, 1899.

5. Of Th. Nöldeke :

Geschichte des Korans, Göttingen, 1860. Das Leben Muhammeds, Hannover, 1863. Geschichte der Perser und Araber Zur Zeit der Sasaniden, Leyden, 1879.

Die Ghassanischen Fursten aus dem Hause Gafna's, Berlin, 1887.

6. Of J. Wellhausen :

Muhammed in Medina.

Reste Arabischen Heidenthums, Berlin, 1897.

Skizzen und Vorarbeiten, Viertes Heft, Berlin 1889.

Die Ehe bei den Arabern, Göttingen, 1893.

Das Arabische Reich und sein Sturz, Berlin, 1902.

7. Syed Ameer Ali : Spirit of Islam.

Syed Chirag Ali, A critical exposition of the Jehad.

Prof. Browne, A Literary History of Persia.

Prof. Margoliouth, Mohammed and the rise of Islam.   Tr.]

II

THE QUR'AN

Qur'an is the Arabic name for the Muslim Bible, or the collection of messages delivered by Mohamed in the name of God, in his capacity as an inspired prophet—messages which, according to him, were now transmitted by the angel Gabriel and now directly revealed to him in visions or in dreams.

Unlike the Bible the Qur'an is not a book arranged according to chronological order, or according to the nature of its contents. It is a motley collection of hymns, prayers, dogmas, sermons, fables, legends, laws and temporary ordinances, with reiterations and contradictions. This is due to the fact that Mohamed did not personally collect the revelations announced by him during a period of twenty-three years. Probably he did not wish them all to be preserved, for a great number of them dealt only with matters of passing importance. So many changes had he effected in his laws and in his teachings that he possibly feared to hand them all down to posterity. Finally he wished, until death, to keep himself free to make necessary additions and alterations. After his death all the fragments of the revelations were put together, even those that were revised or repealed.

Verses of the Qur'an, scattered in all directions and recorded on parchment, leaves, stones, bones and other rude materials, or those that were preserved in the memory of his contemporaries— all, indeed, were collected together and divided into chapters— large or small—without any regard to chronology or their contents. Thus arose the Qur'an with all its imperfections as we know it.

Only by a careful examination of the life of Mohamed and the language of the Qur'an are we able, to a certain extent, to fix the date of its individual *Suras*. With the help of the Arab biographies* of Mohamed, of which some go back to the second century of the Hegira, we are able to determine the dates of those sections of the Qur'an which refer to historical events. Where such is not the case the determining factors are the form and the contents of the revelations. In the beginning Mohamed appears as a reformer, later as the founder of a new religion, and finally as a ruler and a law-giver. In the first period he was entirely carried away by an overpowering enthusiasm. His language is rhythmical. It bears a true poetical colouring. In the second period cool calculation takes the place of excited imagination. He is rather rhetorical than poetical. His language is sober and well-reasoned, and it springs forth no longer, as before, from the heart with warmth and spontaneity. In the third period the language falls absolutely flat. It is insipid, not only when laws are laid down, directions issued, or accounts of wars related, but also when he describes the omnipotence of God, the beauty of the world, the terrors of the Day of Judgment, and the splendour of Paradise.

Abu Bakr was the first to collect the Qur'an. The reason for the collection is said to have been the death of many literate persons in the war against the false prophet Musailama, and the fear that soon there might be none left who understood or knew the Qur'an by heart. A certain Zaid Ibn Thabit† who had served as secretary to the Prophet was commissioned to collect the revelations. When he had done his work he made it over to the Caliph, from whose hands, on his death, it passed on to his successor, Omar, who in turn left it to his daughter Hafza, the widow of the Prophet. Zaid's work was nothing more nor less than a transcript of the scattered fragments, regardless of any

---

* [See, Sprenger's Life of Mohamed (in English). Tr.]

† [See, Das Leben und Die Lehre des Mohammad. Sprenger, Vol. III pp. xviii et seq. Tr.]

order or division into chapters. This collection was not the official version, for there were other fragments still in circulation, which differed more or less from it and which led to disputes as to the correct reading of particular passages. To put an end to this position of affairs, fatal alike to the laws and the unity of the faith, the Caliph Othman ordered a fresh redaction of the Qur'an—its basis being the collection under the Caliph Abu Bakr.

On its completion the Caliph sent a copy to all the chief cities of the provinces, and ordered the destruction of other versions which differed from it. The division of the Qur'an into 114 chapters dates from the time of the Caliph Othman, but, as already mentioned, the division was effected without reference to its contents or to any chronological order.

As regards the arrangement, it was chiefly designed with a view to its length—the longer sections being placed in the beginning, the shorter at the end. Since then Othman's Qur'an has passed for the authorised version of the divine revelation, and although later readings came into existence, differing from each other, owing to further copies having been made—these can be traced back to the defectiveness of the Kufic writing which remained in use for several centuries and in which not only the vowel signs were wanting but also the diacritical marks which serve to distinguish letters similar to each other.

As to its contents, it is, as already mentioned, of a very mixed character. It includes not only the whole of his teachings and his legislation, but also a considerable portion of his life, an account of his temporal and spiritual warfares, as also the history and the sayings of the prophets who had gone before him.

If we would arrange the Qur'an chronologically we must begin with those revelations which deal with the mission of Mohamed, his spiritual wrestlings, resulting in the conviction that he is truly called by God to fight against the superstition of

33

5

his people, and to enthrone in the place of idolatry the worship of one all-powerful, all-knowing God who punishes the wicked and the unfaithful frequently enough in this life, but always for certain in the next, and also rewards the good and the faithful. To this may be added his attacks upon his opponents who despised him and declared him a liar, and the words of consolation which God addressed to him to cheer him on in the path of endurance and perseverance.

Many *suras* of this period paint the joys of Paradise and the terrors of Hell with a brush deeply dyed in material colours, and portray the terrible catastrophies which will herald the Day of Judgment. Others contain prayers, hymns, imprecations and so forth.

To these *suras*, mostly short ones—bearing the impress of passionate excitement—follow somewhat longer ones containing further explanation of individual articles of faith, or rhetorical embellishments of numerous legends of the older people and the prophets, with the object of inspiring courage in his followers and terror in his opponents. In fact Mohamed identifies himself with the former prophets and puts into their mouths words such as he addressed to the Mekkans. They too are stated by him to have been misjudged by their contemporaries until truth triumphed and the sinners were put to shame and perished. To this period also belong further polemics against disbelief which called for miracles from the Prophet in support of his divine mission. But he always referred to the inner truth and the outward perfection of his revelation as the surest sign of its divine origin. Moreover to this period also belong several visions in which the genii paid homage to him, as well as the wonderful account of his mid-night journey to Jerusalem, the passage to heaven which many of his contemporaries regarded merely as a dream, several precepts of an ethical nature, and attacks on the Christian doctrine of the Trinity and the cruci-fixion of Christ. Over and above these there was a great deal of repetition of what had already been said before about God, prophecy, immortality and the future life.

The revelations delivered after his flight to Medina constitute the conclusion of the Qur'an. There, in lengthy *suras* and protracted verses, in which nothing survives of poetry save the rhyme, there are to be found elaborate discourses directed against the Jews and the hypocrites of Medina, who like the Mekkans before, secretly ridiculed and opposed him. There, are to be found an exposition of the laws of war, and a history of the various campaigns conducted against the Jews and the heathen. Victories are atributed to divine aid—mishap to want of trust in God. In between are to be found many laws of ritual, many legislative enactments of a civil and criminal nature, called forth by the necessity of the moment.

As we are not writing here a Muslim *Jus Canonicum* we will content ourselves only with those laws and articles of faith which have been of some consequence in the development of the Muslim people. Recognised as the Qur'an is, as the basis and foundation of Muslim law and theology, it must not be forgotten that many individual doctrines and laws are of later growth.

After the death of the Prophet the Muslims themselves felt that a book like the Qur'an, without systematic sequence with all its repetitions and contradictions, oblivious of many important dogmas and laws, would hardly suffice to serve as a guide in all matters theological. By theology the Muslims understood all matters dogmatic, ritualistic and juristic. They had, at first, recourse to the traditions of the Prophet orally handed down, and to the examples of his public and private life *(Hadith* and *Sunnah)*, but when this source, easy as it was to keep it going, failed them, they turned to the decisions of the *Imams*, *i.e.*, Caliphs; for they were the spiritual chiefs of Islam. Upon the basis of the Qur'an, the tradition, the decisions of the *Imams*, there arose, with the aid of analogy and deduction, a still more stately edifice, including within its circumference politics, laws, rituals and dogmas, which, under the Abbasids, was cast into its final shape.

Four chief schools of theology and law arose in Islam, each bearing the name of its founder. They attained the highest authority. The text book* composed by each of these founders serves, up to the present day, as the basis of theology and jurisprudence. These four schools were those of the Hanafites (called after Abu Hanifa b. 80 A.H.; d. 150 A.H.); the Malikites (called after Malik Ibn Anas b. 90 A.H. or 95 A.H.; d. 177-178 A.H.); the Shafites (called after Mohamed Ibn Idris Al Shafii b. 150 A. H.; d. 204 A.H.) and the Hambalites (called after Ahmad Ibn Hambal b. 164 A.H., d. 241 A.H.). These four teachers, known as the Sunnites, are regarded as orthodox, because they acknowledge the same fundamental basis of religion, though they differ from each other on minor points. They consider sacred the traditions of the Prophet and the decisions of the first Caliphs, as explaining and supplementing the Qur'an, in opposition to the Shiites, or the supporters of Ali and his race, who reject many of the traditions coming from the opponents of Ali, and deny a binding force to the decisions of the Caliphs outside the family of Ali, for such they condemn as usurpers.†

In the first century of the Hegira even the most important articles of faith, such as the theory of God and Providence, did not pass wholly unchallenged. They gave birth to most contentious debates. We can scarcely expect a clear cut system

---

* [No legal writings of Abu Hanifa have reached us, nor does he seem to have himself cast his system into a finished code. That was done by his immediate pupils, and especially by two, the Qadhi Abu Yusuff who died in A. H. 182, and Mohamed Ibn al Hassan who died in 189 A. H. See, Macdonald's Muslim Theology, pp. 65-117; Goldziher, Die Zahiriten, pp. 13 et seq.; see, the chapter on Mohamedan law [in] Von Kremer's Culturgeschichte des Orients. It has been translated into English by Khuda Bukhsh.]

† [In Polak's Persien (Das Land und seine Bewohner) the reader will find all the points of difference between the Shiahs and Sunnis very carefully noted, vol. I. 329 et seq. Tr.].

of theology from a man such as Mohamed; a man wholly destitute of intellectual training.

Later, therefore, when, in consequence of contact with the Persian religion and Greek philosophy, there was awakened among the Arabs a speculative spirit and an overpowering thirst for knowledge—the simplest article of faith led to violent discussion or permanent schism. Mohamed required of all his followers belief in one, all-present, all-powerful, invisible, all-wise, all-knowing, just, merciful God—the Creator and the Preserver of the universe.

However simple this view of divinity—it opened to every possible sect a wide battlefield, which grew wider as philosophic studies extended more and more; for every acquisition in this field was made to serve some theological doctrine which had to be traced back to the text of the holy Qur'an. Even in the earliest period some of the orthodox views relating to the character of the Deity and His relation to mankind, as also the views relating to the Qur'an, appeared to many Muslims blasphemously polytheistic. These thoughtful Muslims, who in the beginning only protested against some of the beliefs of the party in power, bore the name of the *mutazzalites*.* They were called so because they rejected the orthodox view. They refused credence to the extreme orthodox view which treated the attributes of God as qualities actually possessed by Him. They, on the contrary, regarded Him merely as the quintessence of wisdom, goodness, power and other attributes.

The theory of divine justice led them further on to the belief in the freedom of the human will; while the orthodox showed a strong leaning towards the doctrine of predestination. As a natural result of the justice of God they believed in different grades of sin and their punishment; while, according to the

---

* [See Browne's Lit. Hist. of Persia, Vol. I, pp. 286 et seq. and Nicholson's Lit. Hist. of the Arabs pp. 206 et seq. Tr.]

orthodox, one who had committed a sin and had died without penance was doomed to eternal hell-fire. From the doctrine of the oneness of God the *mutazzalites* naturally concluded that the Qur'an was *created*, because otherwise they would have had to accept that the two had co-existed eternally.

The orthodox, on the other hand, maintained the eternal character of the Qur'an, otherwise God being eternal the Qur'an would not be regarded as part of God's essence. On any other assumption the whole doctrine of the divine revelation would be undermined, as it in fact was actually undermined, since the *mutazzalites* denied the divine origin and the absolute inspiration of the Qur'an.

We should not, however, consider the doctrine of the divine decree destroying the freedom of the human will, as at all countenanced by the Qur'an—though a large section of the orthodox Muslims so regard it. This doctrine was meant to inspire confidence, to overcome cowardice, to inculcate submission to the will of *Allah*, to serve as a warning against the pride and haughtiness of prosperity, rather than to paralyse human activity or to destroy the freedom of human volition. We must interpret those individual passages of the Qur'an in which a certain carelessness is extolled as a virtue, as intended to discourage too great an anxiety regarding oneself to the neglect of the higher duties of serving God through virtuous practices. Thus the entire religious system of Mohamed, founded on hope and fear, proclaims itself against the doctrine of absolute predestination. In his system the fate of man beyond the grave is made dependent on his religious belief and on his own personal actions.

He who seeks the world, says the Qur'an, to him shall we give forthwith according to our will, but in the life to come he will be ridiculed, rejected, and he will burn in hell. In another passage it says—Enjoy the best things that have been sent down to you ere punishment overtakes you and you no longer

find any help; before the soul calls out: woe to me! I have
sinned, and I have belonged to the triflers, or if God had guided
me I would have feared Him, or if I could only return to the
earth once more I would act righteously. Not so! my signs
(*i.e.*, the Qur'an) reached you, but you declared them to be lies.
You were arrogant and unbelieving.

Again there are passages in the Qur'an which suggest that
man, so far as virtue and belief are concerned, is only a blind
instrument of Divine caprice. Thus it says: for those who are
unbelieving it is immaterial whether you warn them or not,
they will not believe. God has sealed their heart, and on their
ears and over their eyes is a veil. Moreover, say the infidels,
why has God sent down no miracles for Mohamed. Say,—
the Lord leaves in error him whom he wishes, and leads those
who turn to Him and believe in Him and in whose heart His
thought finds a place. Very often the words occur: "God
leads whom He wills and leaves in error whom He wills."

These and similar verses are to be interpreted as meaning
that it rests with Divine Wisdom to confer Its gifts, at whatever time and to whatever people, It pleases; that It strengthens
faith in those who have the tendency to do good; while, in those
who have an inclination to evil, It lets them have their own way,
which takes them deeper and deeper into wickedness and corruption.

Mohamed could not possibly accept the rigid doctrine of
predestination as it was conceived by many Islamic and Christian sects, for the Qur'an knows nothing of original sin, and it
frequently opposes the idea of responsibility for another's sin.
Without the doctrine of original sin an unconditional predestination would come into conflict with the justice of God. According
to the Qur'an Adam and Eve were driven from Paradise on
account of their disobedience, and the human race, by reason
of the victory of human passion over Divine command, was

condemned to mutual hatred and perpetual discontent. But when Adam repented of his sin, God again showed mercy to him, for He said : "Leave paradise. But My guidance will come to you. He who will follow it will have nothing to fear and will never be afflicted. The unfaithful, however, will declare our signs as lies. They will be the eternal companions of hell." The mercy of God is expressed in His revelations. To be saved, faith in the revelation and regulation of conduct according to it, is a necessity.

We have already observed that the history of the earlier prophets fills a considerable place in the Qur'an. The history of the old Testament is adorned with many Jewish legends of a later time, so selected as to suit the purposes of Mohamed. We cannot go exhaustively into the history of the prophets, as narrated in the Qur'an, but we will not pass by what the Qur'an tells us of Christ.

Christ was the living Word and the Spirit of God, in opposition to the dead letter and the cold formality into which Judaism had fallen in the Middle Ages. For Mohamed the miraculous birth of Christ was by no means extraordinary. Since Adam also was created by the word of God. Mohamed readily believed the miracles related in the Gospels, for the earlier prophets, such as Abraham and Moses, were also said to have performed such miracles. Even the journey to Heaven was nothing new to him. Enoch and Elias were said to have performed such a journey. But he could not give his assent to the belief which exalted a prophet and his mother to the rank of divinity. He accordingly set it down as a wicked invention of the priests. No more could he accept the crucifixion of Christ, because it militated against the justice of God, since no man could suffer for the sin of another—moreover, it stood in opposition to the history of the other prophets whom God rescued from every peril and danger.

According to the Qur'an, therefore, it was not Christ who was crucified, but an unbelieving Jew whom God invested with the figure of Christ.

Just as the legend of Abraham assumed a special importance for Mohamed both on account of Abraham's simple doctrine and on account of the relation in which he stood to the Arabs through Ishmael (and the monuments at Mekka that reminded them of him); so in the same way the legend of Christ was of good service to him chiefly on account of the Paraclete whom Christ had announced, and whom Mohamed might think or at least pretend himself to be.

Besides the prophets of the Bible the Qur'an mentions some others who appear in the old Arab traditions. According to the Shiite belief the prophets were men, pure, perfect and free from sins. The Sunnis, on the other hand, do not believe even Mohamed to have been free from sin, though, they say, he was pardoned by God.

As regards the doctrine of Predestination the Shiites incline more towards the *mutazzalites* and seek to reconcile predestination with free-will. Their most important article of faith is the doctrine of *Imamat*, *i.e.*, the sucession of the descendants of the Prophet, to the Caliphate, through Ali. *Sunnis* reject this view and regard the Caliphate merely as a political institution, founded for the welfare of the people.

Let us now turn to the practical theology of Islam which the Muslim jurists divide into two main parts : the religious ceremonial laws, which include a great deal and which we would describe as Constitutional Law, and Civil Law, which includes police regulations and the law of crimes.

To the former belong not merely rules regarding purity, prayer, fasts, pilgrimage, forbidden food and drink, but also rules relating to the taxes that are to be paid, and the uses to which they are to be applied. The civil law includes (1) the

41

6

commercial laws, (2) the law of wills and succession, (3) the law of marriage, (4) the law of crimes and procedure, (5) the law of war, and (6) the law relating to slaves.

We will pass over the first two sections as beyond the sphere of our work, and will observe as to the third that Mohamed laid down a good many laws for the protection of the wife as against the caprices of her husband. The wife is unconditionally to obey her husband. She is to live so secluded that not a shadow of suspicion of unfaithfulness is to fall on her. Should she fulfil these obligations she is justified in expecting good treatment from her husband. Outside the *harem* conjugal fidelity was enjoined on the husband as a duty. Within the *harem* the law forbade preferential treatment of one wife to the prejudice of another.

Mohamed would not and indeed could not put an end to polygamy. He, however, limited the number of wives to four. Before him, specially in Medina, the practice was to have as many as 8 to 10 wives. As regards four wives, only such could marry as had the means to keep them in comfort. Mohamed further protected women from the relatives of their deceased husbands, who until then had inherited them as chattels.* Of the Mohamedan law of crime we shall only mention here that a wilful murder was punished with death, that it was open to the nearest relatives to whom belonged the right of blood-revenge either to call for the execution of the murderer or to condone it by the receipt of hush-money. An unintentional killing could only be atoned for by payment of the amount legally fixed, which in the case of a woman was only half; in the case of a Jew or a Christian one-third; in the case of a heathen five-tenths. For mutilation there was either the hush-money or the blood-revenge. In the cases of adultery, sodomy, apostacy, the law

---

* [Robertson Smith, Kinship and Marriage in Arabia. pp. 104, et seq. Tr.]

awarded capital punishment. For drinking wine the punishment was 40 stripes. For the first offence of theft the right hand was cut off, for the second the left foot, for the third the left hand, for the fourth the right foot. The law of slaves constitutes the most humane portion of the Islamic legislation. Manumission of slaves was an act, says the Qur'an, most pleasing to God, and was regarded as an expiation of many a sin. Before God, the Qur'an proclaims their equality with freemen, and an authentic tradition tells us that he who manumits a believing slave can never be condemned to hell. Slave girls who give birth to children by their master received their freedom on his death. The children, of course, were born free. They could not be the slave of their father. Even as to the mother his powers were limited. He could neither sell nor give her away as present. A slave could by arrangement with his master obtain his freedom; that is, by indemnifying him. During the period fixed for the redemption the master lost proprietory rights in the slave.

Mohamed could no more abolish slavery than he could abolish polygamy, but he restrained its abuses and recommended manumission.

Oh Ye people, says the Qur'an, we have created you from one man and woman, and have divided you into different classes and tribes so that you might see (without regard to position or descent) that only the most God-fearing among you is the most worthy in the sight of God. In another passage which contains the essence of Islamic teachings, the Qur'an says: Righteousness is not that ye turn your faces to the east and to the west, but righteousness is this: Whosoever believeth in God and the Last Day and the angels and the Book and the prophets: and whoso, for the love of God, giveth of his wealth unto his kindred and unto orphans, and the poor and the traveller, and to those who crave alms, and for the release of the captives, and whoso observeth prayer and giveth in charity; and those who, when they have covenanted, and who are patient in adversity and hardship, and in times of violence ; these are the righteous and they that fear the Lord.

As Mohamed did not belong to the ruling party in Mekka, and as the largest portion of his early supporters were slaves or men of humble vocation in life, it was but natural that he should attack aristocratic prejudices, and proclaim the equality of men, specially of the faithful, as a religious principle.

We will conclude this chapter with a description of the personal appearance of the Prophet as given to us by the Arab biographers.

Mohamed was of middle stature. He had a large head, a thick beard, a round face with red cheeks. His brow was broad and noble, his mouth well-shaped, his nose high and slightly aquiline. He had large black eyes, a vein passed from his forehead over his brow, which used to swell, when he became angry. On his lower lip he had a small mole. His hair descended to his shoulders and unto death retained its black colour. He sometimes dyed it brown and frequently moistened it with fine-scented oil. Only on the occasion of his last pilgrimage did he have it shaved off. Every Friday before the prayer he cropped his moustache, shaved off the hair under his arm, and paired his nails. Most graceful indeed, was his neck which like a silver pole, rose over his broad breast. Between his shoulders he had a mole—reports differ about it—which the Muslims regarded as the seal of prophetship. His hands and feet were very large, but he had so light a gait that his feet left no traces on the sand.*

[*Bibliography.*

1. Geschichte des Qorans, by Th. Nöldeke (Göttingen, 1860).
2. Einleitung in den Koran, by G. Weil (2nd Ed. Bielfeld, 1878).
3. Le Koran, La poesie et Les lois, by Stanley. Lane-Poole (Paris, 1882).

* [See Muir's Life of Mohamed, Vol. II,p. 28;Vol. IV,p. 302 et seq. Tr.]

4. New researches into the Composition and exegesis of the Qur'an, by Hirschfeld (London, 1902).

5. Nöldeke's essay, 'the Koran' in 'Sketches from Eastern History' pp. 21-59.

6. Macdonald's Aspects of Islam. Lecture III, pp. 77-118.

7· The Qur'an, translated into English, with notes and a preliminary discourse, by G. Sale (London, 1734).

Sale's translation is still serviceable. Mention may also be made of the English versions by J. M. Rodwell (London and Hertford, 1861) and by E. H. Palmer (the best from a literary point of view) in Vols. VI and IX of 'The Sacred Books of the East' (Oxford 1880).

8. Nicholson's Lit. Hist. of the Arabs pp 141—180.

9. Syed Ahmad Khan's Essays on the Life of Mohamed.

10. L'Esprit Liberal Du Coran by Benattar. Paris 1905. Tr.   ]

III

THE ELECTIVE CALIPHATE IN MEDINA.

1. ABU BAKR.

Mohamed, who issued laws and directions regarding quite unimportant questions and ceremonies, maintained as regards the constitution of the state the profoundest silence. The unbiassed reader can scarcely find the smallest hint in the Qur'an as to how the newly-founded Islamic Empire was to be governed after his death. Not only as an inspired prophet did Mohamed fail to give any direction as to the most important branch of the law of the constitution, but even as a temporal ruler he made no arrangement as to how and by whom the Arabs whom he had reduced to subjection were to be governed. No other reason for this silence can be suggested or accepted than his desire to avoid all reference to his death. Many faithful, even if they did not perhaps take him to be immortal, still expected that his end would be something extraordinary, as with Christ and other prophets. And even Omar would not believe in his death until an improvised verse of the Qur'an, unknown to him, was cited, which spoke of the mortality of the Prophet. This verse is said to have been revealed after the battle of Ohod, at which Mohamed was taken for dead and the faithful had lost all courage and all confidence. It runs thus : Mohamed is a mere messenger of God. Many have died before him. Should he die a natural death or were he to die in battle—would you turn away from him, *i. e.* would you become disloyal to him ? If this and similar verses of the Qur'an had really been revealed earlier—this fact at least proves this much, that besides Abu Bakr, who was anxious to exhort the Muslims to remain firm in their loyalty to God and to his Prophet, no one else remembered that in the later years of the Prophet's life any mention was ever made of his death.

Perhaps Mohamed made no arrangements about his successor because he wished to give offence to no party. On one side were his daughter Fatima and her husband Ali, and on the other was Abu Bakr. The dictates of affection pointed to Ali, but sober judgment marked Abu Bakr out as the more suitable successor. Only on his sick-bed is Mohamed said to have expressed a desire to leave some instruction behind, but the intensity of the fever prevented him from carrying out his purpose, and thus he died without making his last will and testament.

Immediately three parties were formed each laying a claim to the sovereignty. At the head of one was Omar*, the later Caliph, who stood out for an elective Caliphate—with the electors and the elected to be sure, of the oldest companions of the Prophet. He anticipated that the choice would fall on Abu Bakr—his friend. The other party was headed by Ali and his uncle Abbas—champions of hereditary monarchy. The third party was the party of the Medinites, who also supported an elective monarchy, but would confine the right of election to their own people, because to their fostering care alone Islam owed its power and its ultimate success. In the capital, at least, the Medinites would have come out triumphant if they had only acted in unity and concert, but as already mentioned the old inhabitants of the town consisted of the tribes of Aus and Khazraj, who from the earliest times fought with each other for supremacy and preferred a foreign rule to the rule of the rival party.† Thus failed the effort of a section of the Medinites to

---

* [See, Prof. Shibli's monograph on the Caliph Omar. Tr.]

† [The whole incident is dramatically described by Von Kremer in his 'Die Entstehung des Chalifats'. See, Vol. I, Chapter I of the Culturgeschichte des Orients. The English translation of this volume is almost ready and thanks to Sir Asutosh Mookerjee will soon be in print. Tr.]

raise their chief—Sa'ad Ibn Ubaid—to the caliphate. While Ali was busy with the burial of the Prophet (who was interred at the very spot where he had died in the house of Ayesha, and which later on was incorporated into the mosque adjoining it), Omar succeeded in securing the election of Abu Bakr. Ali protested in vain, and only gave in after the death of his wife. But Sa'ad left for Syria, and said when called upon to render homage: "By God! I will not do homage until I can discharge against thee the last arrow from my quiver; until I dye the point of my lance with thy blood; until my arms become too feeble to wield the sword against thee."

Bitterly contested as it was, the Caliphate, at this time, was more a burden than a desirable position.

Mohamed had spread his faith more by bribery, cunning, deceit and force than by conviction. After his death, therefore, it was abandoned in many provinces. Ayesha's own words are these: "When the Prophet of God died, the Arabs cast away their faith, the Jews and Christians raised their head, the hypocrites concealed their hypocrisy no longer, and the Muslims looked like a forlorn herd in a cold wintry night." To stifle the disloyalty of the tribes, of whom some reverted to their old freedom, others to the worship of their old ancestral idols, or lent ear to the newly arisen prophets and prophetesses, there were needed close cohesion of the faithful, the imperturbable wisdom of Abu Bakr, and the unbending energy of Omar. The danger was so imminent that even Omar quailed before it. Omar, otherwise so severe and energetic, counselled Abu Bakr to win the Beduins over by exempting them from the poor-tax; a tax by reason of which they had broken away from him. Here Abu Bakr showed himself the stronger and more resolute of the two. He rejected the advice with indignation. He was determined above everything to adhere to the revelation with undeviating constancy, and to fight any one who would by a hair's breadth depart from it.

With the death of the Prophet revelations had ceased and therefore no change or modification could be made in them. He pledged himself to govern his subjects in strictest conformity with the divine laws, and called upon the people to be the judges of his government. He addressed the following words to the crowd assembled to do him homage, and he faithfully adhered to them unto death :—

"O ye people! you have chosen me your Chief Magistrate though I am not the most excellent among you. If I act righteously—deny me not your co-operation. If I do wrong—oppose me. Truth begets trust—untruth leads to treason. I will treat the weakest among you as the strongest until I have vindicated his right, and I will treat the most powerful among you as the weakest until he abstains from unrighteousness. Obey me so long as I obey God. Should I act contrary to the command of God and his Prophet—you are released from your oath of allegiance."[*]

So scrupulous was Abu Bakr that although Medina itself was encircled by hostile tribes and could only be protected against attacks by defensive measures, he nevertheless despatched the expedition against the Syrian borders planned by the Prophet. Until the return of the troops he could only confine himself to measures defensive. Thus by well considered sorties he beat back the rebels in the neighbourhood of Medina. After the return of the troops he appointed a number of commanders to crush the rebels spread over the Arabian Peninsula. These commanders were assisted by the tribes still loyal to Islam and the flower of the old Arab troops composed of the *Muhajarin* and *Ansar*. Khalid, one of the first of the generals appointed by Abu Bakr, directed his attention against the false prophet

---

[*] [See Khuda Bukhsh, Essays : Indian and Islamic. The Essay on 'The Islamic Conception of Sovereignty'. See Nöldeke's suggestive and scholarly article in Vol. 52 of the Z. D. M. G., pp. 18 Sqq. Tr.]

Tulaiha who, like the Prophet Mohamed, announced his divine revelation in rhymed prose, and to whom the tribe of Asad and its allies had rendered the oath of allegiance. He compelled him to fly to Syria and repeatedly defeated the tribes attached to him. Thereafter he fought the false prophet Musailama who ruled the province of Yamama and inflicted on his supporters a crushing defeat.

While Khalid, as faithless and bloodthirsty as brave, was dealing a fatal blow at Musailama, the most dangerous enemy of Islam, the other generals were quelling the rebellion in the province of Bahrain, in the coast-land of the Persian Gulf, which in consequence of the death of the Prophet had rejected Islam, in Oman where a false prophet had arisen, and in Yaman where, on account of the poor-tax the yoke of Islam had been thrown aside.

Thus by the end of the XIth year of the Hegira rebellion had completely been stamped out of Arabia, and Abu Bakr, loyal to the mission of the Prophet, could think of extending the rule of Islam beyond the confines of his native country.†

---

† [I place here the chronology of the Saracen conquest of Syria and Egypt. It is taken from Prof. Bury's edition of Gibbon, Vol. V, pp. 540-543. "The discrepancies in the original authorities (Greek and Arabic) for the Saracen conquests in the Caliphates of Abu Bekr and Omar have caused considerable uncertainty as to the dates of such leading events as the battles of the Yermūk and Cadesia, the captures of Damascus and Alexandria, and have led to most divergent chronological schemes.

I. Conquest of Syria. Gibbon follows Ockley, who, after the false Wākidi, gives the following arrangement :—

A. D. 633 Siege and capture of Bosra. Siege of Damascus. Battle of Ajnadain (July).
,. 634 Capture of Damascus.
,, 635 Siege of Emesa.
,, 636 Battle of Cadesia. Battle of the Yermūk.
,, 637 Capture of Heliopolis and Emesa. Conquest of Jerusalem.
,, 638 Conquest of Aleppo and Antioch. Flight of Heraclius.

Khalid received orders to proceed against the province of Iraq, on the lower Euphrates and the Tigris, then forming part of the Persian empire. Its inhabitants were, to a large extent, of Arab origin and were governed by Arab princes acknowledging Persian suzerainty. Here the fight was no longer, as it was in Arabia, with the people, but it was a fight with the Persian troops who, for a long while, had not known what

---

Clinton (Fasti Romani, II, p. 173-5) has also adopted this scheme. But it must certainly be rejected. (1) Gibbon has himself noticed a difficulty concerning the length of the siege of Damascus, in connection with the battle of Ajnadain (See p. 424, n. 73).

(2) The date given for that battle, Friday, July 13, A.D. 633 (Ockley, I., p. 65), is inconsistent with the fact that July 13 in that year fell on Tuesday.

(3) The battle of the Yermūk took place without any doubt in August, 634. This is proved by the notice of Arabic authors that it was synchronous with the death of Abu Bekr; combined with the date of Theophanes (Sub A. M. 6126), "Tuesday, the 23rd of Lous (that is, August)," which was the day after Abu Bekr's death. The chronology of Theophanes is confused in this period; there is a discrepancy between the Anni Incarnationis and Indictions on one hand, and the Anni Mundi on the other; and the Anni Mundi are generally a year wrong. So in this case, the Annus Mundi 6126 (=March 25, A.D. 633 to 634) ought to be 6127; the 23rd of Lous fell on Tuesday in 634, not in 633 or 635 or 636.

(4) The capture of Damascus in Gibbon's chronology precedes the battle of the Yermūk. But it was clearly a consequence, as Theophanes represents, as well as the best Arabic authorities. Khalid who arrived from Irāk just in time to take part in the battle of the Yermūk led the siege of Damascus. See Tabari, ed. Kosegarten, ii., p. 161, seq.

(5) The date of the capture of Damascus was Ann. Hij. 13 according to Masūdī and Abū-l-fidā, in winter (Tabari); hence Weil deduces Jan. A.D. 635 (See Weil I, p. 47).

On these grounds Weil revised the chronology, in the light of better Arabic sources. He rightly placed the battle of the Yermūk in August, 634, and the capture of Damascus subsequent to it. The engagement of Ajnādain he placed shortly before that of the Yermūk, on July 30, A.D. 634, but had to assume that Khalid was not present. As to the battle of Cadesia, he accepts the year given by Tabari (tr. Zotenberg, iii., p. 400) and Masūdī (A. H. 14, A. D. 635) as against that alleged by the older authority Ibn Ishāk (ap.

victory was,—for since the invasion of the emperor Heraclius, the Persian Empire, owing to aristocratic feuds, civil war, famine, and female rule, had grown feebler and feebler.

Khalid marched from Yamama with 2000 men, but by the time he had crossed the frontier of Iraq he could count 18,000 under his banner; for the prospect of plunder had brought the Arabs round him—some to fight for God and his Prophet, others to reap a rich harvest of booty.

Masūdī) as well as by Abū-l-fidā and others (op. cit. p. 71). Finlay follows this revision of Weil :—

A.D. 634. Battle of Ajnadain (July 30). Battle of the Yermūk (Aug. 23).
„ 635. Capture of Damascus. (Jan). Battle of Cadesia (Spring).
„ 636. Capture of Emesa (Feb). Capture of Madain.
„ 637—8 Conquest of Palestine.

As to the main points Weil is undoubtedly right. That the conquest of Syria began in A.D. 634 and not (as Gibbon gives) A. D. 633, is asserted by Tabari and strongly confirmed by Nicephorus (p. 99, ed. de Boor). The Saracens began their devastation in A. M. 6126 = Ind.7. A. M. 6126 is current from A. D. 633, March 25 to A. D. 634, March 25, and the 7th Indiction from A.D., 633 Sept. 1; to A. D. 634, Sept. 1 the common part is Sept. 1, A. D. 633, to March 25, A.D. 634; so that we are led to the date Feb., March, 634, for the advance against the Empire. In regard to the capture of Damascus it seems safer to accept the date A. H. 14 which is assigned both by Ibn Ishāk and Wākīdi (quoted by Tabari, ed Kosegarten, ii., p. 169), and therefore place it later in the A.D. 635.

The weak point in Weil's reconstruction would be the date for the battle of Ajnādain, as contradicting the natural course of the campaign marked out by geography, if it were certain that Ajnādain lay west of the Jordan, as is usually supposed. The battle of the Yermūk on the east of the Jordan naturally preceded operations west of the Jordan. This has been pointed out by Sir William Muir (Annals of the Early Caliphate, p. 206—7), who observes that the date A. D. 634 (before the Yermūk) "is opposed to the consistent though very summary narrative of the best authorities, as well as to the natural course of the campaign, which began on the east side of the Jordan, all the eastern province being reduced before the Arabs ventured to cross over to the well-garrisoned country west of the Jordan." Muir accordingly puts the battle in A.D. 636. But there seems to be no certainty as to the geographical position of Ajnādain, and it must therefore be regarded as

According to the direction received from the Caliph he wrote forthwith to the commander-in-cheif of the Persian troops :—

"Accept Islam and you are saved, pay tribute and receive for yourself and your people our protection. Otherwise you have only yourself to blame, for I will advance towards you with an army which loves death as you love life."

By these words Khalid intended to encourage the truly faithful to encounter the enemy with an absolute contempt for death and with an assured certainty of a life of everlasting

---

possible that it lay east of the Jordan, and was the scene of a battle either shortly before or shortly after the battle of the Yermūk. The reader may like to have before him the order of events in Tabari ; Mr. Stanley Lane-Poole has kindly supplied me with the references to the original text (ed. de Goeje).

Abū Bekr sends troops into Syria (A. H. 13), I. 2079.

Khalid brings up reinforcements in time for the Yermūk, 1., 2089.

Battle of the Yermūk, 1., 2090 sqq.

Battle of Ajnādain (end of July, 634), 1., 2126-7.

Battle of Fihl (Jan., Feb., 635) 1., 2146.

Capture of Damascus (Aug., Sept., 635), 1, 2146.

As to the date of the capture of Jerusalom Weil does not commit himself ; Muir places it at the end of A.D. 636 (so Tabari, followed by Abū-l-Fidā, while other Arabic sources place it in the following year). Theophanes, under A. M. 6127, says : "In this year Omar made an expedition against Palestine ; he besieged the Holy city, and took it by capitulation at the end of two years." A. M. 6127 = March 634—635 ; but as the Anni Mundi are here a year late the presumption is that we must go by the Anni Incarnationis and interpret the A. M. as March, 635-636. In that case, the capitulation would have taken place at earliest in March, 637—if the two years were interpreted strictly as twelve months. But the words in the text may be used for two military years, 635 and 636 ; so that the notice of Theophanes is quite consistent with Sir Wm. Muir's date. The same writer agrees with Weil in setting the battle of Cadesia in A. H. 14, with *Tabari*, but sets it in Nov. 635, instead of near the beginning of the year. Nöldeke in his article on Persian History (in the Ency. Brit.) gives 636 or 637 for Cadesia. Muir's arrangement of the chronology is as follows :—

A.D. 634 April, the opposing armies posted near the Yermūk. May and June, skirmishing on the Yermūk. Aug. (23), battle of the Yermūk.

happiness. Mohamed had revealed, to be sure, quite a number of verses in the Qur'an, calculated to stir his followers to deeds of a most daring character.

"Believe not," says the Qur'an, "that those who perish in the path of God are dead, they live and will be taken care of by the Lord. They are blessed with His mercy and they will receive with joy those that follow them."

These and similar verses which acquired more and more popularity with the masses were not merely conventional expressions. They urged them on to heroic acts and may be regarded as a very important item, among the causes, which led to the rapid growth of the Islamic Empire—however much the

---

A.D. 635. Summer, Damascus capitulated; battle of Fihl. November, battle of Cadesia.

„ 636. Spring, Emesa taken Other Syrian towns, including Antioch, taken. Heraclius returns to Constantinople. Spring, battle of Ajnādain. End of the year, Jerusalem capitulates. Summer, siege of Madāin begins.

„ 637. March, capture of Madāin.

„ 638. Capture of Caesarea. Foundation of Basra and kufa.

II. Conquest of Egypt. Our Greek authorities give us no help as to the date of the conquest of Egypt, and the Capture of Alexandria, and the Arabic sources conflict. The matter, however, has been cleared up by Mr. E. W. Brooks (Byz. Zeitschrift IV., p. 435 sqq), who has brought on the scene an earlier authority than Theophanes, Nicephorus and all the Arabic histories,—John of Nikiu, a contemporary of the event. This chronicler implies (Mr. Brooks has shown) that Alexandria capitulated on October 17, A.D. 641 (towards the end of A. H. 20). This date agrees with the notice of Abū-l-Fidā, who places the whole conquest within A.H. 20, and is presumably following Tabari (here abridged by the Persian translator); and it is borne out by a notice of the 9th Century historian Ibn Abd al Hakam (Weil. 1. p. 115, note). Along with the correct tradition that Alexandria fell after the death of Heraclius, there was concurrent an inconsistent tradition that it fell on the 1st of the first month of A.H. 20. (Dec. 21, A. D. 640) ; a confusion of the elder Heraclius, with the yonger (Heraclonas) caused more errors (Brooks, loc. cit., p. 437); and there was yet another source of error in the confusion of the first capture of the City with its recapture, after Manuel had

love of war and greed of booty, natural to the Beduins as well as the inner decay and corruption of the Persian and Byzantine Empire, may have contributed to that end. The Persians were not so deeply demoralized as to yield to the victors at the first onslaught. They fought repeatedly against the troops of Khalid—though unsuccessfully—and lost, in the first year of the war, under the reign of Abu Bakr the whole of the country situated on the western banks of the Euphrates, together with the towns of Anbar* and Hira—whence Khalid extended his excursions over the whole of Chaldea and gathered immense booty from the state treasury. Just as he was preparing to cross the Euphrates once again to carry the war right into the heart of Mesopotamia he received orders from Abu Bakr to join the Syrian army which urgently needed his help. In the spring of the year 634 as the number of the volunteers, anxious to avenge the defeat at Muta,† had grown considerably, the

---

recovered it in A.D. 645 (loc. cit., p. 443). Mr. Brook's chronology is as follows:—

A.D. 639 Dec. Amru enters Egypt.

" 640 C. July. Battle of Heliopolis.

" C. Sept. Alexandria and Babylon besieged.

" 641 April 9, Babylon captured.

Oct. 17. Alexandria capitulates.

As to the digressive notice of Theophones Sub Anno 6126, which places an invasion of Egypt, by the Saracens in A.D. 638, it would be rash, without some further evidence, to infer that there was any unsuccessful attempt made on Egypt either in that year, or before A. D. 639. Tr.]

* [Anbar was taken in A. H. 12 (634). For a short time it was the seat of the Caliphate. Abul Abbas Al-Saffah (132-136=750-754) made Anbar his residence and was buried there. His successor Abu Jafar Al-mansur resided in the town until the foundation of Baghdad in the year 145 (762). After this the importance of Anbar gradually diminished. To-day the site of Anbar is quite waste; the situation of the town is indicated by the ruins of Tell Akhar and Ambar in which latter form Ritter already recognised the old name of the town. See Ency. of Islam. Tr.]

† [Bury, Later Roman Empire, p, 262, vol. II. Tr.]

Caliph sent several battalions to the frontier of Syria and Palestine to win, as he hoped without much resistance, fresh laurels for Islam. The times were propitious; for the Byzantine Cæsar, since the Persian war, was stricken with a paralysis of imperial energy; the Arab inhabitants of the frontier were offended by unreasonable parsimony, and the Christian population were inflamed into passion by gubernatorial spoliation and ecclesiastical oppression. The first expeditions of the three commanders, who individually attacked Syria from three different points, were attended with little success, and not until Khalid had arrived with a reinforcement of 9000 men and taken over the supreme command did things begin to brighten for the Muslims. As the most important events occurred in the reign of the Caliph Omar we will revert to them in the sequel. Abu Bakr died of fever at the age of 63 (22nd August, 634 A. D.) Mindful of the trouble which the question of succession had occasioned on the death of the Prophet, Abu Bakr, when he felt the end near at hand, thought of deciding the question in favour of Omar.* He sent for the most important and influential companions of the Prophet and put forward before them Omar as the most competent and the most suitable man to direct the affairs of the state. Then he collected the chiefs of the people and made them take an oath that they would acknowledge the successor appointed by him. This being done he appointed Omar. But when the announcement of this choice caused anxiety in some quarters, on account of the severity of Omar, Abu Bakr said:—Omar was so severe because I was too weak. When he rules alone he will be milder than I, for often has he tried to appease me when he noticed that I was inclined to be hard, verily I know that his interior is better than what seems from his exterior.

---

* [Ranke, Weltgeschichte, vol. V, pp. 110 et seq. Tr.]

Abu Bakr's private life was as irreproachable as was his public life. Nothing indeed, could be suggested against him except that he was too indulgent towards Khalid. But that was an act of political wisdom. He used the treasures, which his generals sent to him out of the booty, for purposes of state and state only. He himself remained as poor as before, and continued for some time even as Caliph to maintain himself by trade and farming until his companions persuaded him to devote himself entirely to government. Then alone did he decide to accept a few thousand *dirhams* a year and a summer and winter suit. He was kind, simple, and pious. As the first collector of the Qur'an, to him belonged the credit of its complete preservation. As a lawgiver he set an excellent example to his successors, for in cases unprovided for in the Qur'an and the traditions of the Prophet he gave decisions in consultation with the jurists; decisions which with few exceptions became binding authorities.*

II. OMAR.

A specially propitious star watched over the infancy of Islam, for it set at the head of the Muslims a man, such as Omar,† who was in fact as Abu Bakr had described him, circumspect and energetic; who, free from every selfishness, had constantly one and one object only in view, and that was the welfare and prosperity of the state; who on account of his genuine piety and conscientiousness as well as his patriarchal simplicity had stood out as an exemplar for all subsequent rulers; and who under the Prophet and the Caliph Abu Bakr wielded a powerful influence. In frugality and economy he even surpassed his

---

* [See, Houtsma's Ency. of Islam, under Abu Bakr. Tr.]

† [Von Kremer in the third chapter of his Culturgeschichte has fully described the political measures of the Caliph Omar. He was the real founder, says Von Kremer, of all those institutions which made the Caliphate for centuries the ruling power of the world. See, also, Geschichte der Perser und Araber Zur Zeit der Sasaniden by Th. Nöldeke pp. 246 et seq. Tr.]

8

predecessor. His food consisted of barley bread and dates or olive, his drink was pure water, his bed a paddding of palm leaves. He owned only two coats—one for summer and one for winter and both were conspicuous by extensive patch works. At the pilgrimages (and he was absent at none) he never used a tent. His garment or a mat fastened to a tree or a pole served to protect him from the burning sun. Thus lived the man who was the undisputed master of Arabia, whose generals, during his reign, conquered the fairest and richest provinces of the Persian and Byzantine Empire. His most earnest endeavour was to do justice, to maintain the purity of the faith, to secure the conquest of the world. He refused to keep any longer at the head of the Syrian troops a man, like Khalid, who had stained his martial glory with murder and debauchery, although it was he who retrieved the honour of the Arab arms at the battle of Yarmuk and settled the fate of of Syria by a decisive victory over the Christian troops (immensely superior in number) which led to the surrender of Damascus, the capital of Syria.

To preserve in Arabia the faith, free from false doctrines, he banished the Christians from Najran and the Jews from Wadi-al-Qur'a, permitting them to take their moveable property with them and allotting them so much land in other countries, of their choice, as they had been dispossessed of. For a similar reason he* decreed as mentioned above, that in all conquered countries the non-Muslims should be distinguished from Muslims by their dress, so that they might be recognized at first sight and treated accordingly. In the rapid diffusion of Islam outside Arabia all Arabs who had fallen away from Abu Bakr and were on that account excluded from participating in the holy war were pardoned, and were distributed partly in the Syrian and partly in the Persian army. Omar could reckon upon those, thus pardoned, to emulate the old troops in bravery and valour—whether from religious conviction or otherwise.

---

* [See, Zaydan, pp. 30-33.   Tr.]

It was indeed high time to reinforce the Arabs on the Euphrates if they were to retain the prizes won by Khalid. Abu Ubaidah, the new Commander, had fought several battles successfully, but was beaten at the battle of the Bridge, near the ruins of Babel, and perished with the majority of his troops. An insurrection in the capital of Persia prevented the total wreck of the Arab troops before the reinforcements. Omar therefore sought to make amends for these losses by new acquisitions. Muthanna, who now took charge of the troops, was again in a position to measure swords with the enemy, and he sent out his cavalry on predatory expeditions to the other side of the Euphrates. But when Yazdajerd ascended the throne the combination against the Muslims became all but universal, and Muthanna had to retire into the desert, where he died in consequence of a wound received at the battle of the Bridge. On the receipt of this mournful news Omar, in the spring of 635, proposed personally to lead an army to Iraq, but his friends dissuaded him from this intention and he appointed Sa'ad Ibn Abi Waqqas as Commander-in-chief, who in the battle of Qadasiyya inflicted so complete a defeat on the enemy that Yazdajerd had to surrender to the Muslims the so-called Arabian Iraq and to confine himself henceforward to the preservation of the provinces, situated to the east of the Tigris with Madain as the capital. Hira was again taken possession of by the Muslims; the fort of Obolla was captured; and the town of Basra was founded which commanded the navigation of the Persian Gulf.

These successes, which secured not only fame and glory but also rich booty and unbounded luxury, attracted more and more troops. The Arab army became so powerful that Yazdajerd left his residence at night without even a show of fight and retired with the remnant of his troops to Hulwan, in the high mountain chains of Media. When Sa'ad entered the abandoned town and witnessed its splendid palaces and pleasure-gardens he recalled to his companions the words of the Qur'an which referred to the Egyptians drowned in the Red Sea but which applied equally well to the Persians. "How many gardens and fountains and cultivated fields have they forsaken and how many places of pleasure and delight in which they were wont to find joy. Neither the heaven nor the Earth mourns for them. All these have we (God) bestowed upon another race."

Sa'ad fixed his headquarters in the white palace* where he sent for the booty consisting of gold, silver, precious stones, weapons and works of art. So immense was this booty that, after deduction of the legal fifth† for the state treasury, there was still enough left to pay 12,000 *Dirhams* to every soldier. At the instance of Omar the Muslims had to leave Ctesiphon and to make the newly-founded city of Kufa, situated on an arm of the

---

* [See, Guy Le Strange, The Lands of the Eastern Caliphate, p. 34. The Great Sasanian palace, of which the ruins still exist on the Eastern Bank of the Tigris, was known to the Arabs under the name of the Aywan-Kisra, 'the Hall of the Chosroes,' and this, according to Yakubi, stood in Asbanbur : while another great building, known as Al-kasr-al-Abyad, 'the white Palace', was to be seen in the old Town a mile distant to the north. This last, how-ever, must have disappeared by the beginning of the 4th (10th) century, for all later authorities give the names of, 'the White Palace' and 'the Hall of the Chosroes' indifferently to the great arched building which to the present day exist here as the sole relic of the Sasanian Kings. This building had a narrow escape from complete destruction in the middle of the 2nd (8th) century, when Mansur was founding Baghdad ; for the Caliph expressed his intention of demolishing the Sasanian palace, and using the materials for his new city. His Persian *wazir*, Khalid the Barmacide, in vain, attempted to dissuade him from this act of barbarity, but the Caliph was obstinate ; the *wazir*, however, gained his point, for when the order came to be carried into effect, the demolition was found to be more costly than the materials were worth for the new building, and the Arch of the Chosroes, as Yakut calls it, was left to stand. At a later period much of its stone work was carried off for the battlements of the new palace of the Taj in East Baghdad, which the Caliph Al-muktafi finished building in the year 290 (903). Tr].

† [One of the most considerable sources of state revenue was the war-booty of which the fifth fell to the treasury. A source (says Von Kremer) which in the almost unbroken conquests of the first century must have brought in immense sums. Tr].

Euphrates, the seat of their Government. Better climate, a splendid strategical position, and the fear of corruption in the old capital of the Persians induced Omar to issue this order. Yazdajerd had soon to continue his flight further north, for Hulwan fell after the victory of Sa'ad at Jalula. The next campaigns were directed, on the one hand, against northern Mesopotamia, resulting in the conquest of Tikrit, Mosul, Harran, Kirkisiya and Roha (Edessa) and on the other against the province of Khuzistan (Susiana), terminating in the capture of Tostar (Shuster) and the surrender of the Prince Harmozan, who to please Omar or to save his neck accepted Islam.

Yazdajerd, in the meantime, did not remain inactive. He stirred on his satraps to present a united front to the Muslims, who showed, more and more, that without limit was their love of conquest.

It was an opportune moment, then, for the Persians, for Sa'ad had been deposed from the governorship of Persia, severe famine had thinned the Syrian ranks, and a portion of the Muslim troops were busy in Egypt.

An army, as strong as had once met at Qadasiyya, assembled in the neighbourhood of Nehavand. This news caused so fearful an alarm at Medina that Omar proposed to take over in person the command of the army, which he had rapidly re-inforced, to march against Persia, but he ultimately appointed Numan Ibn Mukrin as Commander who inveigled the enemy, by a feigned flight, to an unfavourable position, and thereby won a complete victory for the Muslims.

Omar took advantage of this victory to push forward his conquests into the interior of Persia. He clearly saw that he must conquer Persia proper if he was to save the troops, stationed at the frontier provinces, from recurring attacks Upon the advice of the captive commander, the Persian Fairuzan, Ispahan, the capital of the Persian Empire, was attacked and was compelled to surrender. Shortly after Hama-dan and Reyy obeyed the sceptre of the Caliph. Other towns were conquered in Farsistan as well as in Kirman and Sijistan. For several years however the fort of Istakhar (Persepolis) offered an obstinate resistance.

The conquests made in the north and east of Persia, under Omar, slipped out of Muslim hands wherever strong Muslim garrisons could not be maintained, with the result that these conquests had to be made over again.* Muslim conquest in Syria, on the other hand, was more firmly planted, because there neither racial nor religious differences were so acutely pronounced.

After the capitulation of Damascus the Muslims, in a few years, under the leadership of Abu Ubaidah, whom Omar appoint-ed in the place of Khalid, subjugated Balbek, Hims, Hamah, Jerusalem, Haleb, Antioch; finally the fortification of Cæsaria and the rest of the towns on the coast of Syria and Palest:ne. The Syrian army then turned to the Euphrates and was soon in possession of the Iraqian Amid and Kirkisiya, in the neighbour-hood of Rakka.

On its subjugation Omar personally undertook a journey to Syria, to issue suitable laws, to regulate the distribution of the land and to protect the inhabitants from acts of violence.

Now was the turn of Egypt † to exchange the Bible for the Qur'an or at least to bow, in humility, to the reverers of the latter.

Personally Omar hesitated and could not easily decide to send out a comparatively small army to the banks of the Nile,

---

* [For Persia, see Dictionnaire de la Perse by Barbier De Meynard. It is a mine of most useful information. For Muslim conquest of Persia, see, (1) Bury's Later Roman Empire. (2) Gillman's History of the Saracens, (3) Benjamin's Persia, (4) Sismondi's Fall of the Roman Empire, Chapters XII—XV. Tr.]

† [See Dr. Butler's Arab Conquest of Egypt. Tr.]

protected as it was by fortified and thickly-populated towns which could by sea count upon the unimpeded support of the Byzantine Government. Omar could not however very well refuse the request of the brave and cunning Amr Ibn Aas, a soldier of tried valour, to proceed with his faithful troops to Egypt.* Amr, indeed, was well aware that if once the first step was taken the honour of Islam and that of the Arab army would compel the Caliph to sanction further measures to prosecute the war. Amr is even said to have travelled early to Egypt. If so, he must have known that the hatred of the Coptic race towards the Byzantine Government was more fierce than was the case in Syria, because ecclesiastical oppression and misconduct on the part of plundering officials were far worse than in Syria. In case of defeat the desert, where they feared no pursuit from the Greeks, offered a safe asylum to the Arabs.

In December 640 Amr started from Syria and with 4000 men whom he had with him he took the frontier fortress of Farma. Then he proceeded unopposed to Bilbis, where he beat back the Christians who fought him, and was soon in sight of the fort of Babylon, on the eastern bank of the Nile, in the neighbourhood of the modern town of Al-Qāhera. In the meantime his small soldiery was re-inforced by the Beduin tribes—also some 12000 men arrived from Medina. Amr was now in a

---

* [The part which Amr played in Islamic history begins with his conversion in the year 8 (629-630). Mohamad sent Amr to Oman where he entered into negotiations with the two brothers who ruled there, Jafar and Abbad b. Julanda, and they accepted Islam. The Prophet died while Amr was in Oman. But he did not remain there long. Probably in the year 12 (633) Abu Bakr sent him with an army to Palestine. In this undertaking Amr played a most prominent part. The subjection of the country west of the Jordan was his achievement and he was also present at the battles of Ajnadain and the Yarmuk as at the capture of Damascus. It is needless to add here any thing more about Amr as Dr. Weil has exhaustively dealt with the conquest of Egypt and the part that Amr played at Siffin and at the arbitration. See Houtsma's Encyclopædia of Islam, under 'Amr.' Tr.]

position to conquer that strong bulwork, the capital Memphis, situated on the western bank.

After the capture of Babylon the Copts concluded peace with Amr who as against a very moderate payment of the ordained taxes assured them perfect religious freedom together with complete security of person and property. Whilst under the Byzantine rule they had to endure all manner of religious and political oppressions. Thus Amr, without drawing his sword from the scabbard, became master of Memphis, and the Greek garrison had no alternative left to them but to retire to Alexandria.

In the spring of 641 Amr, supported by the Copts, started for Alexandria, beating back the Greeks at every turn, with a view to lay siege to it, and did, in point of fact, besiege it. Heraclius made every effort to save Alexandria, whose loss would seriously affect not only Egypt, the granary of Constantinople, but the rest of north Africa. On his death, when in consequence of troubles arising from disputed succession and mutiny of soldiers, Alexandria lay utterly helpless—it was not very difficult for Amr to take by storm the already prostrate town awaiting its impending fall. At the express order of Omar, however, the town was treated with a marked leniency.

Amr wanted to make his residence on the other side of the Nile, but Omar would not consent to his governor residing at so great a distance from Medina. Thus at the spot where Amr had pitched his tent during the siege of Babylon the new town of Fustat was founded which remained the seat of the governor until the Fatimides built the new town of Al-Qāhera in the XIVth century of the Hegira. By making the old canal navigable they restored connection with the Red Sea so that henceforward Arabia might easily be supplied with provisions from Egypt.*

---

* [It is the canal which leaves the Nile at Fustat, intersects Cairo and opens into the Red Sea at Kulzum (the Klysma of antiquity). Nero, Trajan

However great the services of Amr to the Caliphate, however earnest his effort to fill the treasury and granary of Medina with Egyptian gold and Egyptian corn—Omar nevertheless treated him with an extraordinary harshness, because he firmly believed that the rich country round the Nile could yield a still greater revenue, and therefore concluded that his governor either treated the inhabitants with undue indulgence or that he misappropriated the larger portion of the income.

He was therefore called upon to render account to a special Commissioner and to surrender to him half of his possessions. Moreover with him in the Governorship was associated Abdullah Ibn Abi Sarh, foster-brother of the later Caliph Othman. With his life, indeed, did Omar pay for his insatiable greed to enrich the treasury more and more at the expense of the conquered Provinces. His governors, to satisfy him, were constrained to levy heavy and offensive taxes. A mechanic, on whom Mughira, the Governor of Kufa, had imposed a daily tax of two silver *dirhams*, travelled to Medina to appeal against this imposition. In his appeal he failed. He therefore attacked Omar with a dagger and inflicted on him several wounds, in consequence of which he died on the 3rd of December 644.*

Like his predecessor Omar before his death determined to settle once for all the question of succession and thus to avert anarchy and civil war. He at first appointed Abdur Rahaman Ibn Auf, one of the oldest companions of the Prophet, as his successor. But he refused the honour. Thereupon Omar nominated six men who were charged with the election of the new Caliph. These were:—Othman, Ali, Zubair, Talha, Sa'ad Ibn Abi Waqqas, and the aforesaid Abdur Rahaman Ibn Auf, by whose casting vote after a protracted discussion Othman was acclaimed ruler of the faithful.

---

and Omar join hands in this work. Events of the most modern times remind us of this. Ranke, Weltgeschicte, Vol. V. p. 154 Masudi, Vol. IV, p. 97. Tr.]

* [Muir's Annals of the Early Caliphate, p. 279.]

9

Omar soon settled his own affairs. He begged his tribesmen to pay some small debts for him which he had incurred, and he entreated Ayesha to allow him to be buried by the side of Mohamed and Abu Bakr. He thus concluded peacefully and with resignation his ten years' reign, which in point of fact however was of yet longer duration, for not only under Abu Bakr but also under the Prophet he had made his voice felt most effectively.

Never was his opinion rejected unless it was too obviously dangerous to the safety of the state. Thus Mohamed did not listen to him when he called for the head of Abdullah Ibn Ubayy,* an influential Medinite, hostile to Islam. Similarly he was not listened to when he demanded execution of the captive Abu Sufyan or when he objected to the conclusion of peace at Hudaibiya. Even Abu Bakr opposed him when he wanted to kill Sa'ad Ibn Ubaid because he would not do homage. We have, however, seen that even Omar could be inconsistent, for he advised Abu Bakr to remit the poor-tax to the rebels ; but, forbearing as Abu Bakr was, he sternly refused his consent to this proposal. Even to the above mentioned Mughira, the governor of Basra, he showed greater indulgence than was expected of him, since Mughira, inspite of all accusations persistently levelled against him, was appointed Governor of Kufa.† Equally indulgent was he towards Abu Musa (the successor of Mughira, to the Governorship of Basra)—who stood charged with embezzlement, corruption and falsification of accounts. In glaring contrast stands his severity not only towards Khalid but also towards his own son, who for drinking

---

* [Before the coming of Mohamed Abdullah had dominion over Aus and Khazraj—the only case, says Ibn Hisham, explicitly in which these two tribes united under a common chief. He accepted Islam but he is regarded by Muslims as the head of the hypocrites (munafikun). Tr.]

† [See Muir's Annals of the Early Caliphate, pp. 264, 265, 268 et sqq.]

wine and immorality was, at the instance of his father, publicly scourged to death.

Omar may be regarded as the real founder of the Islamic Empire, for to him owe their origin the most important institutions which give permanence to government. He not only rewarded the warriors but also anxiously looked after those that they left behind. He appointed judges for the conquered provinces. He fixed the pay of the different officers. He established a government secretariat and founded a department of finance. He ordered a census to be made and the property of fellow citizens to be valued and appraised. He thus introduced order into the system of finance and taxation. Finally he fixed the Mohamedan era which dated from the flight of Mohamed to Medina. *

III. OTHMAN.

The deliberation, which ended with the election of Othman, lasted three days, for with the exception of Abdur Rahman lbn Auf the rest of the nominees of Omar were men fond of power, who urged their own claims to the Caliphate. When Abdur Rahman saw that, he asked the claimants, one after another, whom they would nominate were they themselves excluded from the competition. Opinion was equally divided between Othman and Ali. Abdur Rahman† thereupon gave his vote to Othman, since Othman promised to govern unconditionally, not only according to the Qur'an and the Hadith but also according to the example and precept of his two predecessors, while Ali would not pledge himself to accept the first two Caliphs as his absolute guide. Othman, however, showed

---

* [See Sachau, Zur Altesten Geschichte des Muhammedanischen Rechts. An appreciation of Omar's fiscal, judicial and administrative measures, p. 705. I hope to translate this invaluable monograph into English at an early date. Tr.]

† [He died in the year 31 (652). Tr.]

himself pliant and accommodating only till the homage was over. It was soon discovered that not only in many points did he depart from the example of Omar, but he even disregarded the divine Law. This, to be sure, provoked a lively discontent among the true believers. The avowed partiality shown by him to his kinsmen in the shape of high appointments and immense donations from the state treasury, did more damage to the Caliph in public estimation than even deviations from the traditions and practices of the earlier days. These kinsmen were mostly men who either personally or whose parents had vigorously opposed Islam, and who, by their immoral conduct, had caused public scandal and had provoked public indignation. Thus gradually passed into the family of Othman immense wealth and tremendous political power—a family which, like that of Abu Sufyan, the arch-enemy of Mohamed, traced its descent from Omayya, while the descendants of Hashim (and the Prophet belonged to this family) were robbed of all influence in the government. This state of affairs embittered both Ali and his party and the power-loving Talha and Zubair. No less indignant was the party of the Orthodox because of the redaction of the Qur'an—their grievance being that it was carried through without their consultation and advice, and that the Caliph had decreed the destruction of all older copies whereby no correction or criticism was possible.*

---

* [Syad Ahmad Khan, in his essay on the Life of Mohamed quotes two traditions bearing on the subject of the compilation of the Qur'an. They are these:—

Zaid Ibn Thabit relates that "Abu Bakr sent a person to me, and called me to him, during the battle with the people of Yamama and I went to him; and behold! Omar was with him and then Abu Bakr said to me, "Omar came to me and said, "Verily a great number of the readers of the Koran have been slain on this day of battle with the people of Yamama, and really I am afraid that, if the slaughter should be severe, much from the Koran will, in consequence, be lost, and verily, I consider it advisable for you to order the Koran to be collected into one [corpus." I said to Omar, "How can I do a

The complaint against Othman grew louder and louder. The discontent became more and more stridently vocal on account of the administration of his unpopular governors, and the feeling of resentment was fed and fanned into flame by Ali, Talha and Zubair, who had a large following in Egypt, Basra and Kufa.

---

a thing which the Prophet has not done ?" He rejoined, "I swear, by God, this collecting of the Koran is the best way." And Omar used to be continually returning to me and saying "you must collect the Koran", till at length God opened my breast so to do, and I saw that what Omar had thought was advisable."

Zaid Ibn Thabit also relates that "Abu Bakr said to me, 'you are a young and prudent man, and I do not suspect you of forgetfulness, negligence, or perfidy; and, verily, you used to write for the Prophet the Revelations sent down to him from above;—then search every place for the Koran, and collect it. I answered, 'I swear, by God, if people had ordered me to carry about a mountain with me from place to place, I should not feel it so heavy as I do the order which Abu Bakr has given for collecting the Koran'. I said to Abu Bakr, 'How do you do a thing which the Prophet of God did not ?' He replied, ' By God, the collecting of the Koran is a good act !' And he used perpetually to return to me, until God opened my breast upon the matter, whereas his and Omar's had been before opened. Then I sought for portions of the Koran, whether written upon leaves of the palm tree, on white stones, or in the hearts of those who remembered them, until I found, in the possession of Abu Khuzaima Ansari alone, the last part of the chapter entitled 'Repentence.' This copy of the Koran then remained in the possession of Abu Bakr until God caused him to die; after that, Omar had it as long as he lived; after him it remained with his daughter Hafsa." (Bukhari).

The copy of the Koran collected by Zaid Ibn Thabit came down in a perfect state to the Caliphate of Othman, who caused numerous copies of it to be taken and distributed among the Muslims. The following is the Hadith which gives full details of this fact. Anas Ibn Malik relates that "There came to Othman, Hudaifat, who had fought with the people of Syria, in the conquest of Armenia, and also in Azarbijan with the people of Irak, and that being shocked at the different ways adopted by people in reading, the Koran, he said to Othman, 'O Othman! Assist this nation before they differ among themselves, in the way of reading the word of God, as much as the Jews and Christians differ. Then Othman sent a person to Hafsa, ordering her to send to him the Koran in her possession, and saying, 'I shall have a number

Only Syria (where Muawiya ruled as governor) was free from mutinous revolutions; since he alone was capable of discharging the duties entrusted to him by Othman. In Egypt, where the party of Ali was strongly represented, it was already taught that Mohamed would some day rise from the dead, and that until then Ali had been appointed his *vazir*. Thus was laid the foundation for the later extravagant doctrines of the *Shi'ites* which even went the length of declaring the *Imams* descended from him as representatives of God on Earth; nay, as a part of the divinity itself.* Probably under the secret guidance of Ali,† Talha and Zubair, and assisted by their gold, the malcontents agreed and resolved to march together to Medina to force Othman to depose his governors. In Egypt Abdullah lbn Abi

---

of copies made of it, after which I shall return it to you! Hafsa having made over the Koran to Othman, he sent for Zaid Ibn Thabit Ansari, and Abdullah Ibn Zubair and Said Ibn Aas, and Abdul-Rahman Ibn Harith Bin Hisham all of whom, except Zaid Ibn Thabit were of the Koraish tribe. And Othman said to the three Koraishites, 'when you and Zaid Ibn Thabit differ about any part of the dialect of the Koran, then do you write it in the Koraish dialect because it came not down in the language of any tribe but theirs! When the above-named Koraishites had done as Othman had commanded, and when the number of copies had been made, Othman returned the original to Hafsa, and had a copy sent to every quarter of the countries of Islam, and ordered all the other leaves upon which the Koran was written to be burned. Ibn Shahab said "Then Kharijah, son of Zaid Ibn Thabit informed me that the former had heard his father saying, 'As I was compiling the Koran I missed one verse of the chapter entitled *"The Confederates."* But verily I heard that verse from the Prophet. Then I searched for the verse, and found it with Khuzaimat Ansari and entered it in the Chapter of *The Confederates.* (Bukhari.) Tr.]

* [See, Von Kremer, Gesch. d. Herrschen. Ideen. pp. 372 et. sqq. See, also Friedlander's The Heterodoxies of the Shiites, and Goldziher's Beitrage zur Litteraturgeschichte der Schi'a. Tr.]

† [Dr. Gustav Weil does not place before us facts which would justify the conclusion that Ali was, as a matter of fact, in any way implicated in the conspiracy against Othman. To my mind, the probability is all the other way. As to Talha and Zubair—their case is entirely different. Tr.]

Sarh, the foster-brother of Othman who, after the recapture of Alexandria, was appointed governor of the entire province in the place of Amr, was to make room for Mohamed, a son of Abu Bakr and a trusted friend of Ali. In Kufa the Omayyad Said Ibn Aas, who was so unwise as to call his province the Garden of the Quraish, was to resign his place in favour of Abu Musa Al Ashari the deposed Governor of Basra. And further Abdullah Ibn Amir, another cousin of the Caliph, was to be removed from the Governorship of Basra.*

Othman received information of the design, and summoned his Governors to Medina to discuss suitable measures to suppress the insurrection. His council could arrive at no common decision, and the Caliph himself, old and wavering, could not adopt a firm line of policy. It is however said that he decided, in accordance with the view of the Governor of Basra, to divert

---

* [No very conspicuous changes were effected during the first year of Othman's reign; for the Caliph Omar, already before his death, had confirmed all the governors in their posts for the following year. Only Mughira Ibn Shuba was recalled from Kufa and Saad Ibn Abi Waqqas appointed in his place. But after the lapse of a year Saad had to retire in favour of Walid Ibn Uqba, brother of Othman on mothers' side. This caused intense dissatisfaction in the circle of older Muslims, because his father Uqba (Weil's Leben Mohammeds, p. 110) was one of the bitterest enemies of the Prophet anp was executed after the Battle of Badr. And yet in the very first year of his Caliphate Othman introduced innovations calculated to inspire doubt and distrust among the people. He increased the pay of the *Emirs* appointed by him and acted in an arbitrary fashion in more ways than one. In the following year (25th of the Hegira = 28th Oct. 645—17th Oct. 646) he dismissed Amr Ibn Aas from the governorship of Egypt and in his place appointed Abdullah Ibn Saad. Difficulties having arisen, however, in Egypt he had to send him back there as Commander-in-Chief. But no sooner was the cloud past and the danger over than he dismissed Amr again and re-appointed Abdullah in his place. Both these appointments; namely, the appointment of Walid and that of Abdullah, provoked a great deal of indignation because, first, they were related to Othman, and secondly they had incurred the displeasure of the Prophet. See for fuller details, Weil's Geschichte der Chalifen, vol. I, pp. 156—160. Tr.]

the activity of the rebels by means of a foreign war, whereby the internal revolution would cease by itself. But Malik-ul-Ashtar,* chief of the Kufans and an instrument in the hands of Talha and Zubair who had placed their wealth at his disposal, frustrated this decision. He went ahead of the Governor† (then proceeding from Medina), occupied with the rebels the approach to Kufa, and compelled him to return to Medina.

To the helpless Caliph no other course was left than to appoint, according to the wishes of Al-Ashtar, Abu Musa as the Governor of Kufa. The Kufans clearly saw that, yielding as Othman was, they would secure their object by making him depose his Governors and setting up in their stead men of their own party. They therefore kept up communication with Basra and Kufa, and before Othman was in a position to oppose them they had carried out the decision formed by them. The overawed Caliph hushed the rebellion into silence by granting all manner of concessions, but scarcely had they withdrawn when he repented of his weakness. The conspiracy extended more and more, and in the following year (35 A. H. 655-6 A. D.) the chiefs of the rebels, with a still larger number, started from Fustat, Kufa and Basra for Medina. Othman had only a few hundred men at his disposal. He was therefore constrained to give in to the Egyptians who constituted the larger portion

* [The Governor of Basra.]

† [Ashtar was loyal companion and lieutenant of the Caliph Ali. At the time of the conspiracy which led to the murder of Othman he brought 200 men to Medina (35 = 655); on being persuaded by Ali's promise of reforms he returned with his companions. He did not take part in besieging Othman's house nor in his assassination either. In the battle of the camel he fought hand-to-hand with Abdullah Ibn Zubair. At Siffin he commanded a corps of 4,000 cavalry and infantry and was in favour of continuing the fight. When Ali proposed him as the Arbiter for his party he was rejected as having been the chief agent in provoking the civil war. He was appointed Governor of Egypt, but was poisoned at Muawiya's instigation . See, Ency. of Islam. Sub "Al-Ashtar" Tr.]

of the rebels, and to appoint the hated Mohamed, the son of Abu Bakr, as the Governor of Egypt. This concession which meant the renunciation of his sovereignty, was not seriously made either by the Caliph or his *vazir* Merwan. They merely desired to get rid of the rebels and hoped, with the aid of troops from Basra and Kufa, to crush further insurrection.

As soon as the Egyptians had withdrawn, a messenger was sent to Abdullah Ibn Abi Sarh with a letter confirming his appointment afresh, and urging him at the same time to chastise Mohamed and his companions. The messenger, a slave of Othman, was unfortunately taken captive and was searched, and when they found that letter on his person, they decided straight away to return to Medina. Othman threw all the blame on Merwan, but he refused to surrender him to the rebels. Othman was thereupon ill-treated in the mosque, and with difficulty managed to escape to his residence which a handful of men secured from surprise. Now he was called upon to resign, but when he declared his willingness to die rather than to surrender the sovereignty entrusted to him by God, his house was besieged and all supply of provisions cut off.

The rebels, reluctant to slay a man gray with years, who like Ali was the son-in-law of the Prophet, and who had sacrificed much for the success of Islam, had hoped to starve him into surrender. But, after several weeks of siege, when they apprehended the arrival of Muawiya with his Syrians for the protection of the Caliph, they adopted extreme measures. They set fire to the gate of his house, and while Merwan was defending the approach to the house of the Caliph the son of Abu Bakr with his followers from another side burst into the chamber of the Caliph. The Caliph was at once killed (17th June 656). For three days his corpse lay uncared for. None ventured to show the last honours to it.* Only on the fourth day some

---

* [D'Ohsson, English Translation p. 472].

10

Omayyads secretly and in all haste brought it to the burial ground, and were content with burying him outside the wall which encircled it.

In spite of the civil war which under Othman afflicted the Muslim empire, war continued abroad, and many successful military operations were conducted by the much maligned governors. In North Africa Abdullah Ibn Abi Sarh extended the frontier of the empire as far as Kairowan.* In Persia, Walid Ibn Uqba, who later, at the instance of Ali, was deposed for drunkenness, reduced the province of Adherbaijan to subjection and also made conquests in Armenia† and Asia Minor where he worked in concert with Muawiya. Further, under Othman, Muawiya conquered the island of Cyprus.‡ Abdullah Ibn Amir chastised the rebels in Fars and conquered Persepolis, then he proceeded to Khorasan§ where Yazdajerd several times, with the help

---

* [Kariowan was founded in 670 by Uqba Ibn Nafi. See, Bury p. 353,, Vol. II, Tr.]

† [It will be convenient to put together here the chief facts regarding the relations of the Arabs to Armenia :—

637. First Saracen Invasion.

639. Saracens penetrate to Tovin, which, however, is soon afterwards lost.

650. Armenia becomes a Saracen Province.

656. Armenians revolt against the Arabs but in 657 return to their allegiance. The country is ruled by tributary Armenian Princes.

686. Romans attempt to recover Armenia and hostilities continue till 693 when the Arabs subject the land and Arab governors are appointed. Bury, Later Roman Empire, p. 322. Vol II. Tr.]

‡ [See, Suyuti, p. 160. Col. Jarrett's Translation, Tr.]

§ [Khorasan in the Middle Ages was far more extensive than is the province of its name in modern Persia. Mediæval Khorasan extended on the north-east to the Oxus, and included all the districts round Herat which now belong to Afghanistan. On the other hand the small province of Kumis, on the northern boundary of the great desert, which at the present day is included within the limits of Persian Khorasan, was of old a separate district, and formed in the time of Mustawfi a province apart. Hamd-Allah divides Khorasan into four quarters (Rub') or districts; namely, Nishapur, Herat, Balkh and great Marv. Tr.]

of the Turcomans, tried the fortune of war, but was eventually killed in flight. The Muslims then advanced victoriously to the Oxus.

IV. ALI, HASAN AND MUAWIYA.

A whole week passed away after the murder of Othman before a successor was appointed. The three leaders of the insurrection, Ali, Talha and Zubair, had hoped that Othman would voluntarily resign, as every one of them had his eye eagerly fixed upon the vacant throne. Either out of faith in his divinely ordained sovereignty or because of the hope of help that he entertained, or possibly because of the belief that they would not dare to kill him—whatever be the real cause— Othman disappointed them in their expectations. The rebels had to smirch and befoul themselves with the blood of the Caliph, and the successor had to receive the crown from hands soiled ꞏꞏith murder and spoliation. This fact accounted for the hesitation on the part of the aspirants to grasp at the throne. Moreover every one of them knew that in the event of success he would expose himself not only to the implacable animosity of the two rivals, but that he would also have to face the opposition of the entire house of Omayya which had secured an increasing influence at Mekka and which in Syria, where Muawiya ruled as governor, commanded a powerful army. Only after a great deal of reluctance and much insistent pressure on the part of the Medinites to accept the Caliphate and thus to end anarchy and civil war, was Ali induced to receive the homage. To avoid the oath of allegiance several influential men left Medina. But Talha and Zubair were compelled by the Egyptians to take the oath of fealty to Ali. Ali's first act as a Caliph could not but be the deposition of the hateful governors if he wanted to show that his opposition to Othman arose not from a desire to obtain power but to remove the existing evils. But such a policy, as might be expected, resulted not only

75

in his own unpopularity but also in the unpopularit ʳ of his whole party. Of the governors whoever could resist ɲim did resist him, and refused obedience to him and called for vengeance for Othman. But this request Ali could not possibly accede to, partly because he was a *particeps criminis* in the conspiracy, and partly because that would mean condemnation of those most devoted to him. Sahl Ibn Hunaif, the governor-elect of Syria, was beaten back from the frontier of Syria by the cavalry of Muawiya. A similar fate befell Ammar Ibn Shihab* who was to take over charge of the governorship of Kufa from Abu Musa.† He was told that before everything else Othman's blood must be avenged. The new governors of Fustat and Basra succeeded in taking up their posts, but they could hardly give their full support to Ali as their attention was diverted to the anti-Ali parties that were formed here and there.

The province of Yaman submitted to the new governor but the out-going officer had managed to empty the treasury, and

---

* [See Muir's Annals of the Early Caliphate p. 268.]

† [Abu Musa belonged to yaman and early accepted Islam. After his conversion he joined the emigration to Abyssinia and only returned on the conquest of Khaibar. Thereupon he was appointed governor of a district by Mohamed. In A. H. 17 (638) Omar conferred on him the governorship of Basra on the deposition of Al-mughira. Then in A. H. 22 (642-643) he was transferred to Kufa—since the people of Kufa declared that they would like best of all to have him as their governor. But the people of Kufa soon grew tired of him. He was re-called after a year and was given back his post in Basra. Some years after Othman's accession he was deposed and Abdullah Ibu Amir was appointed in his place. Abu Musa, thereupon, settled in Kufa. In A. H. 34 (654-655) Othman appointed him governor of Kufa; but when on the murder of the Caliph this town joined the cause of Ali, Abu Musa was forced aside and had to flee. Once again he appears in the history of Islam as one of the two arbitors appointed after the Battle of Siffin (37 A. H.=July, 657) to decide as to whether the sovereignty belonged to Ali or to Muawiya. Here Abu Masa was outwitted as we will learn in the sequel. This arbitration was the end of Abu Musa's political activity. According to the oldest tradition he died in Kufa in A. H. 42 (662-663) or in 52. Houtsma's Ency. of Islam Tr..]

thereby to enrich the enemies of Ali, who withdrew to Mekka and there declared him to be the murderer of Othman and preached rebellion. At their head stood Talha and Zubair who had fled from Mekka, as well as Ayesha, the widow of the Prophet, whose hatred of Ali was far more intense than was her love for her brother Mohamed, the leader of the Egyptian rebels and the real murderer of Othman. Ali at first proposed to hasten to Mekka to suppress the insurrection in the holy town, but his enemies had repaired to Basra where, so strong was the party of Talha and that of the expelled governor, Abdullah Ibn Amir—the two having combined together—that they had hoped to take possession of the town without much serious effort and then to form an alliance with the Kufans against Ali.

The governor Othman Ibn Hunaif could not prevent Ayesha from occupying a portion of the town with her people, but he vigorously resisted her when she openly preached insurrection. Nor indeed were people wanting who blamed her unwomanly conduct and set down Talha and Zubair as traitors and leaders of the insurrection against the Caliph Othman.

By deceit and treason these i.e. Talha and Zubair, managed to drive away the governor of Ali, but in doing so they completely forfeited the public esteem and confidence, and none but a few of the people of Basra joined them when it actually came to a battle with Ali.

Ali left for Basra when he learnt that Ayesha had gone there with her followers. He had some 900 men with him, and this is an eloquent commentary on the scant sympathy which he found with the Medinites. He halted at the frontier between Arabia and Iraq and sent messengers to Kufa to summon the auxiliaries from there. At first Abu Musa, the dismissed governor, strove to win the Kufans over for Talha, but when he failed in his effort he tried to make them at least indifferent spectators of the war. In the Mosque where Ali's invitation was read out he declared that the dispute between Ali and his rival was a purely secular dispute which they might settle as best they could; that the true believers need not worry themselves about it; that only so long as Othman was alive was it their duty to take up arms on his behalf and for his protection.

Not until Ali had sent his son Hasan, the grandson of the Prophet, to Kufa and had promised to make Kufa his home, after victory was won; not until several eloquent and influential men had pointed out, on the one hand the right and the claims of Ali, and on the other the necessity of rendering him help to put an end to dispute and division; not until then did 3000 men hasten to the camp of Ali. To these, in the meantime, several thousand joined from various parts of Arabia, and Abu Musa was driven out of Kufa by Malik-ul-Ashtar.* Strong as Ali was to attack the enemy in Basra he yet, to prevent further bloodshed, entered into negotiation with them, and was weak enough to exclude from his troops men who had taken part in the murder of Othman, for Ayesha had made this a condition precedent to any negotiations whatever. These rebels now apprehended that for the sake of peace they would be sacrificed or at least shelved.

Before day-break, before any final arrangement had been arrived at between Ali and Ayesha, they attacked the hostile troops. Treason! Treason! was the cry on all sides. And thus when the day dawned there was a formal battle, which is known as the "battle of the camel" because Ayesha, seated on a camel, led the centre of the Basran troops and urged them on to fight until Talha and Zubair had fallen, until her camel became lame and she was taken captive.†

---

* [Müller, Der Islam im Morgen—und Abendland, I, 301—304, 309, 317, 319—327, 331, 345. Tr.]

† [The full name of Zubair was Abu Abdullah Zubair, son of Al-Awwam, son of Khuwailid, son of Asad Al-Quraishi Al-Asadi. He was the nephew of Khadija, the first wife of the Prophet. Historians agree in saying that he was one of the first to accept Islam and the first to draw sword on behalf

Ali, however, treated her with every consideration and sent her back to Medina with a strong escort. He did not treat the town of Basra, when he entered it on the following day, as one conquered by the sword, for he tried to win over the hearts of the Iraqians to enable him to conquer with their aid the still remaining dangerous rival Muawiya.

True to his promise he repaired to Kufa and prepared for war.

Muawiya, on the other hand, was not inactive during the six months which elapsed between the murder of Othman and the subjugation of Basra. Having a large army at his command he could have saved Othman if he had so intended, but he remained listless and apathetic at Damascus. Probably he too was aiming at the Caliphate and he anticipated that Ali and his confederates would soon disagree and fall out. He therefore made the fact of the murder of Othman the basis of a strong agitation. His blood-stained shirt was publicly exhihited in the mosque and all blame was fixed upon Ali, who was present in Medina and stood in intimate relations with the rebels, who later even filled the most important place in his army. As many of the leaders of the Syrian troops belonged to the family of Othman it was easy

---

of Mohamed. In the wars of the prophet he took a prominent part. Even after the death of the Prophet he enjoyed considerable influence. In the misunderstanding between Ali und Ayesha he took the side of Ayesha but in a half-hearted fashion. He perished in the battle of the camel in the year 36 of the Hegira.

Talha, son of Ubaidullah, son of Othman, son of Amr, son of Kab At-Taimi was one of the noted companions of the Prophet. He took part in all the early wars of Islam and was one of the most influential men after the death of Mohamed. He was one of the first ten converts to Islam and one of the those whom Mohamed had assured the joys of paradise. The Caliph Omar, when about to die, nominated him one of the commission which was to decide the question of succession to the Caliphate. He found him very proud and that was the reason why he would not nominate him as his successor to the Caliphate. He died in A.H. 36 (656 A.D. See, Al-Fakhri, French translation, p. 137 notes 2 & 3. Tr.]

enough for him to urge them on to avenge Othman, and thus he could, with perfect confidence in his army, reply to the messengers of Ali, who from Kufa several times summoned him to render obedience to him, that he would not submit until the murderers of Othman had received the punishment they deserved.

Between law and anarchy, which Ali had called forth or at least had encouraged, between the heathen principles of blood-revenge and self-help and the precepts of Islam to which Ali had appealed and by which he in a certain measure had justified the insurrection against Othman, the transgressor of the Laws of the Prophet; finally, between the old Mekkan aristocracy which had found its exponent in Muawiya, the son of Abu Sufyan, and the idea of hereditary monarchy to which Ali had clung as the nearest kinsman of the prophet—war was now invitable.

In April 657, with an army of some 7,000 men, Ali started from Kufa and crossed the Euphrates at Rakka. From Syria alone Muawiya mustered more troops than Ali did from the rest of the provinces put together. The Syrian army was a model of discipline, while the army of Ali, composed of men from various countries, showed a lamentable lack of discipline and organisation. This situation was aggravated by his incessant reference to divine right, as also by his stern and unbending spirit, which stood in striking contrast to the pliant and engaging manners of Muawiya. On the plain of Siffin, a few miles above Rakka, on the western banks of the Euphrates, the two armies lay facing each other. Several months rolled away in negotiations, single combats and petty skirmishes. Neither of the two contending armies wished to precipitate the war, which offered neither the prospects of great booty nor the hopes of paradise, as had been the case with the earlier wars against the unfaithful, which inspired alike love for battle and contempt for death.

The two armies had followed their leaders to the battle-field, and had resolved to fight for them; but at heart they were for a

peacefl l termination of the dispute, for despite all the eloquence ol Ali and Muawiya who sought to give a religious colour
to the war, most of the combatants felt that they were being
sacrificed rather in the interest of power and ambition than in
the cause either of the State or of their faith.

As the two chiefs of the army (both of whom were aspiring
to the Caliphate) could not agree—there occurred, at last, a fearful
battle (25th of July) which, with fluctuating fortune, lasted for
three days. There, as once at Badr and Ohod, Ali fought with
youthful courage and energy. On the third day, when the aged
Ammar Ibn Yasir,* one of the oldest and most influential
companions of the Prophet, stirred the Iraqians on to fight, the
battle became fiercer than ever. He called out to them:
"Follow me, ye companions of the Prophet. The gates of heaven
are open, the *Houris*, richly adorned, are ready to receive us. Let
us conquer and meet Mohamed and his companions in paradise."
With these words he flung himself into the very thick of the
battle and fought until he succumbed to his wounds. This not
only roused the troops of Ali to vengeance but also produced a
depressing effect upon the Syrians. Even the descending

---

* [Ammar, a partisan of Ali, is reckoned among those who denied their
faith under torture, but received pardon from Mohamed. He was one of the
emigrants to Abyssinia and took part in the Hegira. He joined the expedition
to Nakhla, as also he did the battles of Badr, Ohod and almost all the
expeditions of the Prophet. In 21 A. H. Omar appointed him successor of
Saad Ibn Abi Waqqas to the Governorship of Kufa and he was given a share
in the command at the conquest of Khuzistan. He was however replaced,
after a year or two, by Mughira. b. Shuba. He opposed the election of
Othman and during his Caliphate he belonged to the opposition. He had
from the outset declared for Ali and according to tradition, withheld from
paying homage to Abu Bakr, for this reason. When the civil war broke out it
was he who won the Kufans for Ali. At Siffin he fought with youthful
ardour. He was deeply versed in the traditions of the Prophet and was greatly
revered for his piety and trustworthiness. He has been encircled by a halo
of most romantic legends by the Abbasid historians. Tr.]

11

darkness of night did not put an end to the carnage, and)n the morning of the 28th of July, the Syrians were so ho)elessly pressed that Muawiya despaired of victory.

To avoid a complete and crushing defeat Muawiya, upon the advice of the cunning Amr Ibn Aas (who after the murder of Othman had repaired to Syria and had joined him), had recourse to a ruse. He ordered his soldiers in the front rank to fasten the Qur'an to their lances, as a sign and token that war should cease and that the decision should be referred to the holy book. The Syrians, under the protection of the Qur'an, now called out to the advancing Iraqians; "Oh! ye faithful, were we to continue to kill each other what would be left of Islam? Who would then fast, pray or fight the infidel? Let the sword rattle no more and let us submit to the divine revelation in which we all believe." This ruse saved Muawiya from a total defeat. Ali saw through it and warned his men not to fall into a trap, for only the fear of a complete defeat had now led Muawiya to appeal to the Qur'an, in which neither he nor his friends Amr or Abdullah Ibn Abi Sarh had any faith. Nevertheless the Iraqians who surrounded Ali (a very few out of respect for the Qur'an, but the majority for love of peace or out of treason) insisted upon the suspension of hostilities with a view to fresh negotiations for a settlement. Ali had to yield (for the traitors threatened his life), and had to stop Malik-ul-Ashtar in the very midst of victory from fighting any more. When Muawiya was questioned as to how he intended to obtain a decision according to the holy Qur'an he proposed that two arbitrators, a Syrian and an Iraqian, should be appointed, with full powers to make over the Caliphate to him who had the most legitimate claim to it according to the law of Islam, and he accordingly appointed Amr as his arbitrator. Ali accepted the proposal, for he could not conceive the possibility of a decision in favour of Muawiya if the decision was actually founded on the Qur'an. The two nominees of Ali were rejected—

Abdull ih Ibn Abbas* on the ground of his kinship with him,
and M lik-ul-Ashtar on the ground that he was the author of
the civil war. Before Ali could think of another the very same
men who had forced him to stop the war shouted out; We will
have no other arbitrator than Abu Musa. In vain did Ali
protest against the choice of a man who hated him because he
had deposed him from the governorship of Kufa, and who even
when in office had betrayed him. Ali at last was browbeaten
into accepting Abu Musa and Amr as arbitrators of his fate and

---

* [Abdullah Ibn Abbas, cousin of the Prophet, is said to have been born a
couple of years before Mohamed's emigration to Medina. A great deal of
legend has gathered around him but we need not pause to consider fictions
invented either by Abdullah himself or by others. He began to come into
prominence under Othman. The Caliph, to whom, according to his own
statement, he was faithful, entrsted him with the leadership of the pilgrimage in the fateful year 35 (655-656) and it was to this that he owed his for-
tunate absence from Medina when the Caliph was murdered. He then went
over to Ali who frequently employed him as an ambassador and appointed
him governor of Basra. All what is related of him after that time must be
accepted with caution, as later on Abbasid party interest or fear of the
Abbasid rulers played an important rôle. Thus he is said to have commanded
a portion of Ali's army at Siffin, which is, however, hardly possible, if he conducted the pilgrimage in the year 35. When Ali was obliged to accept arbitration, he wanted to make Abdullah his representative but his own followers
refused to accept this arrangement. Nevertheless he accompanied Abu
Musa and was in Dumat at Jandal with him. But one fact is confirmed on
all sides; *viz.*, that he took a large sum of money (some say 6 million Dirham)
from the state treasury of Basra and then left the town. There seems to be
a divergence of opinion as to, when this happened—before or after Ali's
assasination. But this is not all, he went over to Muawiya and got him to
secure the stolen sum for him as reward for his treachery. The fact
that after Hasan's abdication he recognised the rule of the Omayyads
cannot be denied even by the Abbasid historians. He died in 68 A. H. (687-
688), or, according to some in the year 69 or 70. But the fame of Abdullah
rests on his knowledge of profane and sacred tradition, of Jurisprudence
and of the Qur'an. He is celeberated as the Doctor of the Comr..unity.
But criticism has exposed him as a conscienceless liar whose forgeries quite
correspond to his political tricks. Only in those rare cases, where there is
absolutely no reason to suspect lying, may his traditions be used for historical
research. Houtsma's Ency, of Islam. Sub Abdullah B. Al Abbas. Tr.]

that of the Empire, and he was even made to consent that n the
treaty that was to be drawn up he was only to be mentiored as
the chief of the Kufans and not the Prince of the Faithful.
Scracely was this arrangement effected (2nd August 657) when
some 12,000 Iraqians banded together and accused Ali of weakness and cowardice and summoned him to confess his fault and
to annul the arrangement.*

The malcontents, whom the Arabs called *Khawarij*,† reckoned

* [See Prof. Browne's Lit. Hist. of Persia pp. 222 et Seq, Tr.]

† [It has been suggested, says Prof. Nicholson (in his Literary History of
the Arabs pp. 209 et sqq), that the name Khariji (plural khawarij) refers to
a passage in the Koran (iv, 101) where mention is made of "those who go
forth from their homes as emigrants to God and His messenger"; so that
'kharijite' means 'one who leaves his home among the unbelievers for God's
sake' and corresponds to the term muhajir, which was applied to the Meccan
converts who accompanied the Prophet in his flight to Medina. Another name
by which they are often designated is likewise Koranic in origin, *viz*, *Shurat*
(pl. of shar): literally 'Sellers'—that is to say who sell their lives in return
for Paradise. The kharijites were mostly drawn from the Beduin soldiery who
settled in Basra and Kufa after the Persian war.........The main-spring of the
movement was pietistic, and can be traced to the Koran readers who made it
a matter of conscience that Ali should avow his contrition for the fatal
error which their own temporary and deeply regretted infatuation had forced
him to commit. They cast off Ali for the same reason which led them to
strike at Othman; in both cases they were maintaining the cause of God
against an unjust caliph. It is important to remember these facts in view of
the cardinal Kharijite doctrines (1) that every free Arab was eligible as Caliph
and (2) that an evil-doing Caliph must be deposed and if necessary put
to death. ....From this it appears that the Kharijite programme
was simply the old Islam of equality and fraternity, which had never
been fully realised and was now irretrievably ruined. Theoretically all
devout Muslims shared in the desire for its restoration and condemned the
existing Government no less cordially than did the Kharijites. What distinguished the latter party was the remorseless severity with which they carried
their principles into action. For the Kharijites; see, Brünnow's Die Charidschiten inter den ersten Omayyaden (Leiden, 1884); Wellhausen's Die religios-
politischen Oppositions parteien in alten Islam (1901); Khuda Bukhsh's
Islamic Civilisation pp. 124 et seq where is translated a passage from De
Goeje's Edition of Frag. Hist. Arab—which sets forth the views of the
Kharijites and shows how those views were met by the Orthodox. Tr.]

among their ranks men of different shades of temper and belief. There were those who sought to sow the seed of dissension ; then there were the readers of the Qur'an who desired the settlement of the dispute through the Qur'an, but did not intend that the decision should be left to two intriguers but to men of wisdom and probity ; finally there were the bold and heroic warriors who had distinguished themselves in the battle of Siffin and who could not forgive Ali for the weakness he had shown in concluding peace contray to his conviction: Before the retreating army of Ali had reached Kufa the malcontents retired to Harura, where they encamped and sent out missionaries to invite support to strengthen their party, but they could not prevent Ali from sending out Abu Musa to the Syrian borders to confer according to the treaty with Amr regarding the question of the Caliphate. *

Ali, to be sure, could not expect anything from the arbitrators appointed. Abu Musa was his enemy, and Amr was an avowed partisan of Muawiya. Amr set up the claim of Muawiya on the score of his kinship with Othman. Abu Musa took exception to this proposition, for to him the Omayyads were even more hateful than Ali was, and urged that if kinship was the determining factor then the son of Othman had a higher claim than any one else. He suggested some other names, but Amr rejected his nominees, one and all. Thereupon Abu Musa said : Since we cannot agree as to the choice of the Caliph the best course for us is to depose both Ali and Muawiya and leave it to the Muslims to choose a Caliph for themselves. Amr assented to this proposal, but after Abu Musa had deposed Ali, Amr called out : You see even the arbitrator appointed by Ali deprives him of sovereignty. In this I am in entire agreement with him but I proclaim Muawiya as the

---

* [The conference took place at Dawmat-ul-Jandal, a place in the Syrian desert just south of the thirtieth degree of latitude, and about equidistant from Damascus and Basra. in February, A. D. 658, Tr.]

rightful Caliph. Abu Musa saw too late that he was overreach-
ed by Amr, who triumphantly returned to Damascus where
Muawiya received afresh the homage of the Syrians.

No one in Kufa was induced by this fraud to accept
Muawiya as Caliph. Abu Musa, despite his hatred for Ali,
protested against it, and when Ali declared the truce at an end
and summoned the Iraqians to battle they hastened to his banner
to fight Muawiya once again.

The *Khawarij* however would have nothing to do with Ali
since he refused to acknowledge his fault. They took up their
position at Nahruwan between Baghdad and Wasit * Ali took
no notice of them and hoped to win them over by kind treatment, as there were among them many genuine enthusiasts whom
he could not very well honestly condemn or find fault with.
But soon their number grew, and they began to ill-treat the
followers of Ali. The Kufan troops in the meantime showed a
refractory spirit, and Ali, while on his way to Syria, was compelled to return again to fight the Khawarij at Nahruwan.
He conquered them without much difficulty, for only some
12-1500 men, the merest fanatics, held their ground and fought
to the last.

Victory notwithstanding—this event was most unpropitious
for Ali, for when after the destruction of the Khawarij he
sought to pursue his march to Syria, the Kufans desired time
for a few days to rest and to supply themselves with provisions.
But, once at home, they refused to go and fight abroad. Thus
Ali was forced to remain inactive at Kufa while Muawiya
extended his rule in all directions. Egypt was the first to pass
under his sway.

---

* [From Harura they advanced towards Mada'in (Ctesiphon) with the
intention of occupying it, but they failed to do so. They then continued their
march to Nahruwan, near the Persian frontier. Tr.]

Ali's governor, Mohamed* the son of Abu Bakr, tried, contrary to the advice of his predecessor, to extort homage from some of the people of Upper Egypt who wanted to remain neutral until the result of the war. He was beaten and driven into the camp of Muawiya Ibn Hudaij who openly appeared against Ali at Fustat.

Ali now sent Malik-ul-Ashtar, with some thousand men, to replace the devoted but unwise Mohamed. But on the way, at the instigation of Muawiya, he was poisoned. The troops which he led returned to Kufa. Thus Amr, whom Muawiya now appointed governor of Egypt, managed to conquer the country all the more easily, since already before his arrival with 5000 Syrians, Mohamed had been driven out of Fustat.

Mohamed even ventured upon a battle, but his troops did not hold their ground, and he was killed in flight. Muawiya's troops now roamed about, killing and plundering along the Euphrates and the Tigris, and even in Arabia itself. In the year 660 not only Mekka and Medina but even the province of Yaman rendered homage to him, so that Ali really ruled over only Iraq and Persia, although his supporters were not slow in making incursions into the territories conquered by their opponents, and even succeeded in re-occupying Medina and a portion of Yaman. This state of mutual slaughter and mutual plunder weighed so heavily on Muslims that three persons swore to kill the three enemies of the Empire:—Ali, Muawiya, and Amr, the authors of all the calamities brought upon the Arabs. Friday the 15th of Ramadhan (January 22, 661) was the day fixed upon, on which Ali, Muawiya and Amr were to be stabbed, while at prayer, in the respective mosques of Kufa, Damascus and Fustat—to put an end to the unhappy wars conducted not only with sword on the battle-field but also in the pulpit with the weapons of mutual curses and imprecations.

* [Tabari Vol. III, p, 692, French translation.]

But only Ali was mortally wounded, and died on the 3rd day (24th January). Muawiya received only a slight wound, and instead of Amr, who on the day in question did not happen to be in the mosque, his representative was killed, whom the assasin mistook for him. Ali died at the age of 63, and according to some reports was buried at Kufa, according to others he was interred in Medina, but probably at the instance of Muawiya he was buried at an unknown spot in the desert, in order that his grave might not become an object of veneration and a centre of opposition in after days. By his sympathy with the insurrection against Othman, as also by raising the leaders of the rebels to the first offices of the State, Ali had trampled under foot the dignity of the Caliphate and had to pay with life for his folly. The chief fault of Ali in the eyes of the *Khawarij* (and among them were men of noble purpose and genuine conviction, as was proved by their constancy and self-sacrifice at Nahruwan) consisted in his accepting the truce and the treaty instead of dying, like Othman, cheerfully at the hands of the rebels. Not only the intriguers and power-seeking men but also the aged companions of the Prophet, men of unsoiled virtue had refused to recognise the claims of Ali to the Caliphate.

We should not therefore readily give credit to the traditions subsequently forged in favour of Ali, nor should we unceremoniously set down Muawiya as a usurper.

Still from credible sources it is clear enough that Ali surpassed not only Muawiya but even Abu Bakr and Omar in his unfailing love of righteousness, in bravery and eloquence. But it was precisely his love of truth to the extent of bluntness that made him many enemies, while Muaiwya by his courtesy and pliancy made more and more friends. Ali owed the veneration, bordering upon worship, not so much to his personal merits as to a systematic opposition* to the Omayyads and the Abbasids, and to

---

* [See, D'Ohsson's General History of the Othman Empire (English Translation) pp. 198 et sqq. Tr.]

the doctrine of the incarnation of the Deity imported from Persia into Islam, a doctrine which was gradually mixed up with the Christian doctrine of the Paraclete with whom popular imagination had identified him. His own and his son's tragic death, as also the persecutions to which his whole family was exposed, awoke a profound compassion and produced a form of deification similar to that of the Persian princes who were regarded as the descendants of a higher being.

In generosity and in simplicity of life Ali fully resembled his two predecessors. Similarly like them he renounced every pleasure of life except continence. After the death of Fatima, in the second period of his life, he concluded six, some say eight marriages, in addition to some 19 slave girls who, according to the then custom, were his concubines.

The supporters of Ali, specially those who on account of his connexion with the Prophet had recognized him as their Caliph and Imam, acknowledged, after his death, his first son Hasan as their sovereign. Even a portion of the *Khawarij* who had condemned Ali on account of his weakness inclined towards Hasan, and showed their willingness to fight for sovereignty on his behalf with Muawiya. But Hasan was a voluptuary to whom a quiet, peaceful life appealed more than sovereignty or martial renown.

It was precisely for this reason that at the Coronation Ceremony he only pledged himself in a general manner to rule according to the Qur'an and the precepts of the Prophet, but he declined to pledge himself, as was required of him, to fight the enemies of Islam unto destruction. Without being guilty of perjury he wanted from the very moment of his accession to reserve to himself the right of renouncing the throne in favour of Muawiya if he was so inclined, and from the very outset, it seems, he was determined to do that as soon as he could obtain from him security of person and sufficiency of means to continue undisturbed the pleasures of the Harem and the duties of his faith. Instead of leading against Muawiya the Iraqians, at the white heat of passion, for the murder of Ali, he remained for months at Madain, probably negotiating terms with Muawiya and exposing the advance guard of the army to the attacks of the Syrians. The defeated Iraqians were so indignant over it that they openly revolted and on their return to Madain maltreated Hasan. Using this as a pretext, he without further delay concluded peace with Muawiya, who, to become the undisputed ruler, willingly offered to pay him a few million dirhams and a yearly stipend, and granted an amnesty to his friends and relatives. As soon as the treaty was signed Hasan disbanded his army and renounced the throne publicly. Thereupon Muawiya made his triumphant entry into Kufa; while Hasan, after a brief rule of six months, retired to Medina (September 661).

Bibliography.

[Besides the books already referred to at the end of the first and second chapters, I may mention here:—

1. The Muruju' l-Dhahab of Masudi. Arabic text with French translation by Barbier de Meynard.

2. Abul Feda's Annales Muslemici. Arabic and Latin by Reiśke.

3. Abul Faraj's History of the Mohamedan dynasties.

4. Al Fakhri's History of the Mohamedan dynasties.

A French translation has been published by Emile Amar (1910. Paris, Ernest Leroux).

5. El-Makin's History of the Saracens with a Latin translation.

Modern Works.

1. Geschichte der Chalifen by G. Weil 3 vols. (Mannheim 1846-50)

2. Annals of the Early Caliphate by Sir William Muir (London 1883)

3. Das Arabische Reich und Sein Sturz by J. Wellhausen (Berlin 1902).

4. Recherches Sur la Domination arabe by G. Van Vloten. (Amsterdam 1894).

5. Prolégomènes d'Ibn Khaldoun, a French translation of the *Muqaddima* by Baron Mac Guckin de Slane, 3 vols. Paris 1863-68.

6. Culturgeschichte des Orients unter den Chalifen by A. Von Kremer, 2 vols. Vienna (1875-77).

The Calcutta University Press will shortly publish an English translation of the first volume of this most scholarly work.

7. Culturgeschichtliche streifzüge auf dem Gebiete des Islams by A. Von Kremer.

An English translation by S. Khuda Bukhsh in his contributions to the History of the Islamic civilisation (Calcutta 1905).

8. Geschichte der herrschenden Ideen des Islams by A. Von Kremer, Leipzig (1868).

9. Jurji Zaydan's History of Islamic civilisation, translated by Prof. D. S. Margoliouth.

10. The Lands of the Eastern Caliphate by G. Le Strange (Cambridge 1905).

11. A. Müller's Der Islam im Morgen und Abendland 2 Vols. Berlin, 1885.

12. Die Chroniken der stadt Mekka Edited by Dr. Wüstenfeld, 4 Vols. Leipzig. (Specially Vol. IV).

13. Sedillot's Histoire des Arabes 2 Vols. 2nd Edition Paris, 1877.

14. Ibn Khallikan's Biographical Dictionary, 4 Vols. (1843—1871).

15. The Kitab-ul-Aghani of Abul Faraj-ul-Isphahani is a veritable storehouse of the most useful information relating to the social, literary and even political conditions of those times. Caussin De Perceval and Von Kremer have very largely drawn upon it but it still offers a rich field for research.

16. Houtsma's Ency. of Islam. Tr.]

IV.

THE OMAYYADS IN DAMASCUS.

Muawiya as the sole ruler.

Although with the resignation of Hasan all opposition to Muawiya did not end, for the Khawarij (who had constantly blamed them both remained loyal to their principles and maintained the right of a descendant of the Prophet to the Caliphate) condemned Muawiya as a usurper both in Basra and Ahwaz; yet it was not very difficult for the Syrians to crush isolated insurrections. The rebellion was, indeed, essentially wanting in a leader to organise, to guide, and to direct it. The only man whom Muawiya feared was Ziyad, the Governor of Persia, an experienced diplomat, a tried general, who governed a people, easily excited into passion on behalf of the descendants of Ali and who, by reason of the proximity of Basra and Kufa to Persia, could easily form alliance with the rebels in Iraq*. The

---

* [See, Le Strange's The Lands of the Eastern Caliphate pp. 24-25. "The great plain of Mesopotamia, through which the Euphrates and the Tigris take their course, is divided by nature into two parts. The northern half (the ancient kingdom of Assyria) consists mostly of pasture lands covering a stony plain; the southern half (the ancient Babylonia) is a rich alluvial country, where the date palm flourishes and the land is watered artificially by irrigation channels, and this for its exceeding fertility was accounted, throughout the East, as one of the four earthly paradises. The Arabs called the northern half of Mesopotamia Al-Jazirah, 'the island,' the southern half was known as Al-Irâk, meaning 'the cliff' or 'shore,' but it is doubtful how this term came originally to be applied; possibly it represents an older name, now lost, or it was used originally in a different sense. The alluvial plain was also commonly, known to the Arabs under the name of As-Sawâd, 'the Black Ground', and by extension As-Sawâd is frequently used as synonymous with Al-Irâk, thus coming to mean the whole province of Babylonia.

greatest effort of Muawiya was, therefore, directed towards securing him to his side. Ziyad, the son of a slave-girl of Abu Sufyan was, on father's side, a brother of Muawiya but, strictly speaking, he was an illegitimate son of Abu Sufyan, for before his birth the mother had passed into another's possession and according to the Mohamedan Law the issue was his in whose house the child was born. As earlier with Hasan, Ziyad now obtained all that he wanted as the price of his submission, and later on, when he had proved himself a true and loyal subject, he secured much more than he had originally asked for. He was permitted to deal with the treasury in Persia as he chose. No account was required of him. He was declared the

---

The frontier between 'Irâk and Jazirah varied at different epochs. By the earlier Arab Geographers the limit generally coincided with a line going north from Anbar on the Euphrates to Takrit on the Tigris, both cities being reckoned as of 'Irâk. Later authorities make the line go almost due west from Takrit, so as to include in Irâk many of the towns on the Euphrates to the north of Anbâr; this, physically, is the most natural division between the two provinces and it crosses the Euphrates below 'Anah, where the river makes a great bend to the southward. The Euphrates was known to the Arabs as Al-Furât; the Tigris they called Dijlah (without the article), a name which occurs in the Targums as Diglath, corresponding to the latter part of Hiddekal, the form under which the Tigris is mentioned in the book of Genesis. When the Moslems conquered 'Irâk in the middle of the 1st (7th) century Ctesiphon, which they called Madâin, on the Tigris, was the chief city of the province, and the winter Capital of the Sassanian kings. The Arabs, however, required cities for their own people, also to serve as standing camps, and three were before long founded namely, Kûfah, Basrah and Wâsit, which rapidly grew to be the chief towns of the new Moslem province, Kûfah and Basrah more particularly being the twin capitals of Irâk during the Omayyad Caliphate.

With the change of dynasty from the Omayyads to the Abbasids a new capital of the empire was required, and the second Abbasid Caliph founded Baghdâd on the Tigris some miles above Ctesiphon (Madain). Baghdâd soon eclipsed all the recent glories of Damascus under the Omayyads, becoming the metropolis of the Abbasid Caliphate and naturally also the Capital City of Irâk, which province now rose to be the heart and centre of the Moslem empire in the east. Tr.]

son of Abu Sufyan and he was adopted by Muawiya as his brother. He was appointed Governor of Basra, later even of Kufa, of the whole of Persia and Arabia and was even probably selected as the future successor of Muawiya.* Ziyad was only too well aware that the Arabs, who since the time of Othman had acquired a certain amount of licence and freedom, were to be yoked afresh to order and obedience and that the lawlessness which had become everywhere the fashion of the day was to be ended once and for all. He cleansed the provinces committed to his charge of political offenders and common criminals, who before him had carried on their malevolent practices with impunity even in Basra itself, but in carrying out his scheme of reform the precepts of the Qur'an and the counsels of the first Caliphs did not wholly appeal to or satisfy him. He introduced an autocratic spirit into the administration and an undue rigour in police regulations. His

---

* [Umayyads and Abbasids by Jurji Zaydan. (Translated into English by Professor Margoliouth p. 10.) The most celebrated case of adoption in Islam was that of Ziyad, "his father's son" into the family of Abu Sufyán, father of Muawiyah the Arabian Sisyphus. The story is told in the histories. Ziyad was the son of a woman named Sumayyah who was in slavery and bore Ziyad to a Greek client of the tribe Thakif, named 'Ubaid. The fact was not generally known, and Ziyad's parentage was generally supposed to be uncertain, whence he was called his "father's son". When Muawiyah became a candidate for the Caliphate and required help, he endeavoured to enroll among his adherents a number of the most sagacious of the Arabs. Among these was Ziyad, whom he determined to adopt. He therefore obtained an affidavit from a wine dealer of Taif named Abn Maryam Al-Saluli, to the effect that Abu Sufyan had come to his tavern and demanded a prostitute, that Sumayyah had been brought by him to Abu Sufyan, and that Sumayyah in consequence gave birth to Ziyád. The best historians disbelieve this story, which they suppose to have been a fabrication of Muawiyah got up with the intention of securing the services of Ziyad, an intention which was realised. Ziyad in consequence came to be called son of Abu Sufyan, after having been called son of Sumayyah, or "his father's son." Ziyad's family continued to count as members of the tribe Kuraish till they were expelled from it by the Caliph Mahdi in 160 A. H., when they were again affiliated to the above mentioned 'Ubaid, and placed among the clients of the tribe Thakif. Tr.]

example was very frequently followed by later Muslim rulers in entire defiance of the Qur'an.

After sunset none was allowed to leave his house. Infringement of this order was punishable with death. The smallest suspicion sufficed for capital punishment. Not the offender alone but his friends and relatives alike suffered with him. The tongue was cut off straightaway if anyone sought the aid of his tribesmen. And with equal swiftness was the man executed who dared to censure Ziyad, to revile Muawiya, or to praise Ali. With the help of a body-guard, consisting of four-thousand men, of whom a half constantly surrounded him while the remainder served as secret spies or public police, criminals were tracked and brought to justice. In consequence of these measures— wise though severe—it was no longer necessary even to lock up the doors at night. Ziyad is even said to have taken upon himself the responsibility of all goods stolen from the borders of India to the coast of the Red-Sea. While Ziyad, and after his death (673 A. D.) his son Ubaidullah, strove strenuously to establish peace and ensure prosperity at home; the generals of Muawiya won military renown abroad. Uqba Ibn Nafi penetrated into the interior of Africa, to the south and to the west alike, but obtained no lasting results. Khorasan was completely subdued by Ubaidullah; the Oxus was crossed and a portion of Bokhara* conquered for Islam. Other generals conquered Mekran, Sijistan, Zabulistan and individual provinces of India. Even in Asia Minor the Qur'an supplanted the Bible. A portion of Cilicia and the island of Rhodes yielded to the Muslim arms, and Constantinople itself was repeatedly besieged, but was only saved by the so-called Greek fire.†

---

* [See Vambery's Bokhara, Chapters II and III. Tr.]

† [Le Strange, The lands of the Eastern Caliphate p. 137. " Three times, infact, under the Omayyad Caliphs was Constantinople besieged by Moslem armies, but the result was in each case disastrous to the assailants, which is

Of far greater moment for Muawiya and the Islamic Empire than these conquests, which to a great extent slipped out of hand, was the fact that Yazid, the Caliph's son, had taken part in these campaigns. Hitherto Yazid had led a life of pleasure and gaiety, but these campaigns had hardened him into activity. And Muawiya could thus conscientiously bequeath the throne to him, with the sure confidence that he would carry on the work in the same spirit in which it was begun by him. To secure the Caliphate for his house and to save the empire, after his death, from fresh civil wars Muawiya, in his lifetime, managed to obtain the succession for his son Yazid. In Syria where the people had long been accustomed to an unquestioning obedience to the will of their rulers, and where the friends and kinsmen of Muawiya were numerous and powerful, such an innovation could pass unchallenged, but in Arabia and Iraq even the friends of Muawiya openly declared themselves against such an arrangement. They declared it to be

---

hardly to be wondered at, seeing that the Bosporus, measuring in a direct line across the mountainous plateau of Asia Minor, is over 450 miles from Tarsus, the base of the Arab attack.

These three famous sieges are : the first in the year 32 (652), under the reign of 'Othmân', when Mu'âwiyah the future Caliph raided across Asia Minor and attempted to take Constantinople, first by assault, and then by siege, which last he had to raise when news came of the murder of the Caliph 'Othmân. The events which followed soon led to the foundation of the Omyyad dynasty. The second siege was in 49(669) when Muâwiyah, established as Caliph, sent his son and successor Yazid against the Emperor constantine IV but the generals were incapable, the Moslem army suffered a crushing defeat, and Yazìd, succeeding to the Caliphate on his fathers' death had to return home. The third and best known attempt against Constantinople was the great siege lasting, off and on, for many years in the reign of the Caliph Sulaymân, who sent his brother Maslamah in 96 (715) against Leo the Isaurian. Of this campaign, which again ended in a defeat for the Moslems, we have very full accounts both from the Arab and the Greek Chroniclers ; and it was in these wars that 'Abd-Allah, surnamed Al-Baṭṭâl, 'the Champion,' made himself famous, who long after, among the Turks, came to be regarded as their national hero, the invincible warrior of Islam.—Tr.]

an imitation of the Byzantine practice, and thus with the greatest trouble and difficulty did Muawiya succeed in making Mekka, Medina and Basra take the oath of allegiance to his son. Among those, who under compulsion acknowledged Yazid as the future Caliph, we might specially mention Husain, son of Ali, who had already strongly expressed himself against the resignation of his brother, and Abdullah, the son of Zubair, who no less ambitious than his father, excelled him in valour, wisdom and steadfastness. During the life-time of Muawiya, however, none of them found any large following. These two, as well as Abdullah, the pious son of Omar, declared that the oath taken by them was wrested from them by threat. But they could not venture to inaugurate an insurrection. Towards Husain Muawiya is said to have counselled his son to adopt a policy of extreme kindness and forbearance, but towards the son of Zubair one of extreme caution and severity. Even as regards the affairs of the various provinces the shrewd Caliph left for his son useful instructions.* In the case of Arabia, the Holy Land, and the seat of his forefathers, he should act with due regard and consideration. The faithless Iraq he should placate and conquer by unstinted bribery and simulated love. Syria, the main-stay of his power, he should treat with care and solicitude. Further he should watch that the Syrian army did not degenerate or demoralise by long residence in other provinces. It was in this spirit of fostering care that Muawiya looked after the empire to the end of his days. He was anxious that it should not again fall into pieces. Ali would scarcely have succeeded, even if he had conquered Muawiya, in saving the empire; for it needed wisdom and strength of character to subdue again the passions unchained after the death of Othman, and to hold the reins of Government with a sure, unfaltering hand. Muawiya was more courteos, more affable, more tactful than Ali. He knew human nature better, and he knew admirably how to use mankind for his purpose.

---

* [See, Al-Fakhri, under Muawiya. A French translation has been published of this most interesting work. Tr].

This is amply illustrated in his dealings with Amr in Egypt; with Ziyad in Iraq. This was the secret of his success. With every wish gratified and every hope fulfilled he, at the age of 78, (April 680 A.D.) peacefully passed away.*

For twenty years he was the Governor of Syria, and for a similar period as Caliph he wielded the greatest influence over the destiny of the Islamic Empire.

II. The Palmy days of the Omayyads from Yazid I to Walid I.

In spite of the precautions taken by Muawiya, his son Yazid could not, without a struggle, secure general recognition as Caliph.† Seeking in his old age, not unlike his friend Amr, to reconcile himself with heaven, Muawiya had forgotten that perjury and breach of faith had long been justified, among the Arabs, by all manner of sophistry, and appeared to them far less sinful than the violation of the most trifling religious ordinance. When, on his accession, Yazid called for a fresh oath of allegiance Husain and Abdullah, the son of Zubair, refusing to do him homage, left Medina and retired to Mekka, where under the shadow of the holy temple, and at great distance from Syria they hoped to find peace and a suitable base for their operations. But Husain was unwise and inexperienced enough to accept the summons of the wavering and treacherous Kufans,‡ to repair to their midst and to allow himself to be proclaimed Caliph. He sent on his cousin Muslim

* [See, French Translation of Masudi's Kitab-Al-Tanbih, p. 392. Tr.]

† [Zaydan, p. 80. The most famous case of an inter-city war at the beginning of Islam was that between the cities of Basrah and Kúfah; in the days of Ali and the Khawárij, Basrah was on the side of Othman, and Kúfah for Ali, while Syria was Umayyad, Al-Jazirah Kharijite, and Hijaz Sunnite. These attachments varied at different times and with different dynasties. Further, with successive political convulsions fresh unions arose: the first, was the bond of descent between Mudar and Yemen respectively; the second, that of country, between the inhabitants of Irâk, Egypt, Syria etc.; the third, that of religion, as between members of the various Islamic sects, Sunnites, Shi'ites, Mu'tazils. Tr.]

‡ [See, Huart's Histoire des Arabs, Vol. I p. 262. Tr].

Ibn Ukail in advance to Kufa to ascertain the general trend of opinion and the exact strength of his supporters there. Muslim found things favourable for Husain, for not only had many influential men declared for him, but also the then Governor Noman Ibn Bashir looked on passively and with indifference at the revolutionary movements there. Husain was accordingly strengthened in his resolution. But while he was making preparations for departure from Mekka, things took a bad turn for him in Kufa. In the place of the weak Noman, Ubaidullah, the son of Ziyad, was appointed Governor. By threat and by bribery he alienated the Kufans from Husain, caused Muslim to be brought out of his hiding place, and had both him and his host Hani executed. Husain was already in the neighbourhood of Qadisiyya when he received information of these mournful occurrences in Kufa. He wanted straightaway to return, but the kinsmen of Muslim desired vengeance for Muslim's death; still cherishing hope that the whole town of Kufa would rise against Ubaidullah when Husain, the grandson of the Prophet, showed himself there. Husain gave in and continued his onward march to Kufa. But the Beduins, who had joined him in the belief that Kufa had shaken off the yoke of Yazid, now deserted him one by one, and he suddenly found himself face to face with the enemy, with none around him except his family and a handful of the Mekkans. Informed by a captured messenger of the approach of Husain; Ubaidullah sent Amr, the son of Saad, with some thousand men to Qadisiyya to bring Husain, dead or alive, to Kufa. On encountering the vanguard of Amr, Husain directed his steps to the plain of Kerbala; for he could not very well effect a retreat across the desert to the other side of the Euphrates, surrounded as he was by his numerous family. Amr, however, pursued him and summoned him to surrrender. Distrusting Ubaidulla, Husain expressed a desire to surrender and to do homage to Yazid on condition that he was sent either to Mekka or to the Caliph at Damascus. Amr thereupon called for fresh instructions from

Ubaidullah, who in reply repeated his earlier message. When Husain was required afresh to surrender and to go as captive to Kufa, he asked for time to consider till the following morning, and used the night in inducing his companions to abandon him to his fate. Hopeless as the position was; for they were cut off from the Euphrates and were encircled by the hostile troops ; they would not yet be guilty of an infamy, such as was envolved in desertion. Possibly there was still a faint, lingering hope that no believing soldier would soil his escutcheon with the blood of the grandson of the Prophet. Thus on the 10th of Mohurram 61 A. H. (10th October 680) began the unequal contest between Husain and his small band of men on the one hand and a considerable army on the other, which regarded him as a faithless, throne-seeking traitor. In spite of the protection of the Qur'an which he sought, like Muawiya, at Siffin, he and his party, were fiercely attacked. As was easily foreseen the battle ended with the death of Husain and all his male companions, among whom were several of his sons and cousins.*

Ubaidullah sent the women and children and the head of Husain to Damascus ; while the trunk was buried at the *Meshed-Husain* where still year by year on the 10th of Mohurram the mournful celebrations take place. Yazid treated the family of Husain with consideration, but was impolitic enough to assign Medina to them as the place of their residence. There the

---

* [Browne's Lit. Hist. of Persia, pp 226—228. Well says Al-Fakhri :—

"This is a catastrophe whereof I care not to speak at length, deeming it alike too grievous and too horrible. For verily it was a catastrophe than which naught more shameful hath happened in Islám. Verily, as I live, the murder of (Alí) the Commander of the Faithful was the supreme calamity; but as for this event, there happened therein such foul slaughter and leading captive and shameful usage as cause men's flesh to creep with horror. And again I have dispensed with any long description thereof because of its notoriety, for it is the most celebrated of catastrophes. May God curse everyone who had a hand therein, or who ordered it, or took pleasure in any part thereof !

already existing indignation against Yazid must have been intensely heightened at the sight of their deep affliction and at the recital of the recent events; for there had the Medinites often and often seen the Prophet fondle and caress the young Husain. Even in Mekka where Husain had resided for long and where he had endeared himself by his piety, the occurrence at Kufa must have provoked a lively discontent against Yazid; despite his attempt to throw on his imperious governor all the blame for the death of Husain. The hypo-critical son of Zubair who, out of envy and self-seeking, had hurried Husain on to his ruin, now affected the deepest sorrow and tried to use the general ill-humour for his own selfish purposes. He had already preached insurrection against the Omayyads and had kept away with his friends from the mosque where the Governor of Yazid prayed. During the life-time of Husain he had not the courage openly to set himself up as a claimant to the Caliphate. But after his death, he played the Caliph; although publicly, out of feigned modesty, he arrogated to himself merely the title " of the Protector of the Holy temple." Yazid was reluctant indeed to inaugurate his reign with a war upon the holy land; fully aware as he was, that that course would necessarily still more alienate from him the sympathy of the faithful. For a full year, therefore, he watched silently the course of events there. Then he sent a message to Abdullah through Noman Ibn Bashir calling upon him either forthwith to

---

From such may God not accept any substitute or atonement : May he place them with those whose deeds involve the greatest loss, whose effort miscarries even in this present life while they fondly imagine that they do well. !"

"The tragedy of Karbala" says Sir William Muir, "decided not only the fate of the Caliphate but of Mahomedan kingdoms long after the Caliphate had waned and disappeared. Who that has seen the wild and passionate grief with which, at each recurring anniversary, the Muslims of every land spend the live-long night, beating their breasts and vociferating unweariedly the frantic cry—Hasan, Hosein ! Hasan, Hosein !—in wailing cadence can fail to recognise the fatal weapon, sharp and double-edged, which the Omayyad dynasty allowed thus to fall into the hands of their enemies?" Tr.]

101

do homage to him or to hold himself in readiness for the Syrian troops to invade Mekka and to bring him in chains to Damascus. But Abdullah remained undaunted, and when the Syrian army did attack the holy territory under the leadership of his own brother Amr (with whom he was on terms of enmity on account of a love intrigue) he drove it back by force, had his brother mal-treated until he died, and when dead he refused to allow him burial in the common burial ground.

As to Medina. When the new governor Othman Ibn Mohamed shamelessly gave himself up, like a Byzantine prince, to a life of pleasure and luxury in a town, accustomed hitherto to a simple, austere religious life, and when several of the Medinites, returning from Damascus, decried Yazid as an irreligious person, devoted to hunting and addicted to wine, women and song, and as such unworthy of the Caliphate—then, even in Medina the mutinous party gained the upperhand. Yazid was publicly deposed in the mosque, and Othman with his Omayyads was turned out of Medina. Yazid saw himself constrained once more to seek safety in negotiations, for the leader of the new expedition died before the expedition had started from Medina, and Ubaidullah who was to proceed against Mekka excused himself on the ground of ill-health. The real reason for the reluctance of Ubaidullah to lead an army to Mekka was the fact of his disappointment in not receiving the promised reward for his victory over Husain.

But when the messenger, a native of Medina, did not obtain a hearing there, he reported to the Caliph that the town could only be made to obey by force of arms. Yazid then applied to the veteran warrior Muslim Ibn Uqba who, though old and infirm, assumed the command of the army intended for Medina, as he was anxious, before his death, to avenge the murder of Othman, whose kinsman he was. At the head of 12 thousand men, who followed him all the more eagerly, since he gave them not only an unusually high pay but also promised them three days' plunder of the conquered town, he started with an assured

victory. Despite all the bravery of the Medinites they were
defeated at Harra, August, 683, in the neighbourhood of Medina,
and despite all their entrenchments the Syrians penetrated into
the town which Muslim, in fulfilment of his promise, abandoned
to the lust and rapine of his soldiery.

It was only after the Medinites had recognised Yazid not only
as their Caliph but also as absolute master of their life and property that Muslim set out for Mekka but died on the way. To
him succeeded Husain Ibn Numair, whom Yazid had already
appointed to fill his place in the event of his death. In spite of
the terrible misfortunes of Medina the son of Zubair continued his
resistance towards Yazid. He, however, at the very first attack
upon the troops of Ibn Numair, saw that he could not meet the
enemy in open battle, but hoped to defend the town from within.
The sudden death of Yazid,* (11th November, 683), and the
probability that a civil war might break out in Syria, induced
Husain to raise the siege and to return without further delay
to Syria. Yazid's reign was far too short to allow us to draw
his full length portrait. Muslim historians call him "Sinful"
because he violated many of the precepts of the Qur'an; because
in his reign a grandson of the Prophet was slain, Medina
plundered, and Mekka besieged. From a political point of
view however Yazid must be acquitted of all blame. It was
only after every attempt to win the rebels over by kindness
and persuasion had failed, that he resorted to extreme measures.
His mother was a Beduin who at the court of Damascus
pined and fretted for the pure, unconventional life of the nomad.
As a true son of the desert Yazid preferred song, games, poets
and dancing girls to men learned in law or versed in traditions.
But it is the latter that have written the history of Islam and
it is they that have ranked Yazid with the scum of humanity.†

* [See, Masudi's Kitab-Al-Tanbih, French Trans. p. 397 note I. Tr].

† [Yazid was a poet of considerable parts. His Divan has been published
in Europe. In Dr. Brünnow he has found an able advocate who, like Dr.

Muawiya II (son of Yazid, 21 years old) was far too weak
to direct the affairs of the Government in such troublous times.
He felt this himself and is said to have been tormented by
doubts as to his right to the Caliphate as against the
descendants of Mohamed. Report has it that his tutor was
a secret partisan of Ali. It is therefore probable that his
death, which took place some few months after his accession,
was not natural but was due to poison administered by one
of his own family. He left no issue and his younger brother
Khalid was at his death only sixteen. By reason of his
minority, another Omayyad was appointed Regent. Supported
by Husain Ibn Numair and Ubaidullah, Merwan was acclaimed
as such by the people of Damascus—the very same Merwan
who was the *Vazir* of Othman and like Muawiyya a great
grandson of Omayya.*

Gustav Weil, acquits him of all blame from a political point of view. The
Mohamedan view of Yazid is much too prejudiced to be accepted in its
entirety. Yazid was the *de facto* ruler. To question his authority was treason,
and the punishment for treason has always been death. Tr.]

*Genealogical Table of the Omayyads

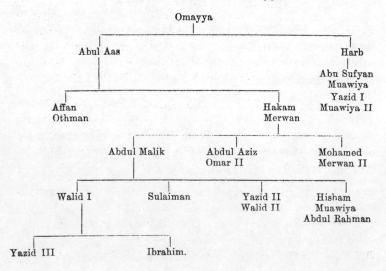

Not merely in Arabia and Iraq had Merwan to face opposition from Abdullah Ibn Zubair* and his party (everywhere indeed

---

* [Abdullah Ibn Zubair, a Quraisite general, who contested the Caliphate of the Omayyads for nine years, was born at Medina in the year 1 (622 A.D.) or according to Waqidi 20 months after the Hegira (shaban 2 = February 624) and was killed in a battle against Al Hajjaj, near Mekka on the 17th Jumada I, 73 A.H. (4th October 692). Compare Wellhausen, Das Arabische Reich und Sein Sturz p. 124. Besides the fact that his father Al Zubair belonged to one of the noblest families of Quraish and was on his mother Safiya's side a cousin of the Prophet Abdullah himself was through his mother Asma, the grandson of Abu Bakr and consequently nephew to Ayesha. According to some muslim authors Abdullah was the first child born at Medina in Islam. While barely 14 Abdullah was present with his father at the battle of Al Yarmuk (14 = 635 A.D.). Three years later he was with his father in the army of Amr B. Al—As who made himself master of Egypt. He played a leading part in the conquest of Africa and in an engagement between him and the *patricius* Gregory killed the latter (29 = 649-650 A.D.). The following year he was with Said b. Al As, in the expedition against Khorasan, and in the same year was one of the theologians appointed by Othman to write down the Qur'an. On the day of the House (18 Dhul Hijja 35 = 17th June 656) Abdullah was one of the most valiant defenders of Othman. At the battle of the Camel (10 Jumada II = 4th December 656) he had the command of his aunt Ayesha's infantry. During the reign of Muawiya Abdullah concealed his ambition for the Caliphate. Only when Muawiya requested him to acknowlege his son Yazid as heir presumptive he refused. On the death of Muawiya Abdullah declared openly against Yazid and refused to take the oath of allegiance. Being informed that Yazid had ordered his head to be cut off, Abdullah escaped at night and set out with Al—Husain for Mekka. By Yazid's orders, Amr b. Al-Zubair, a brother of Abdullah and hostile to him, was sent at the head of an army against Abdullah. But the latter defied his brother's forces, Amr was taken prisoner and died under the rod.

Abdullah, however, feared the rivalry of Al—Husain and treacherously advised him to undertake his journey to Kufa, which was sure to be fatal for him. Directly the news of Al Husain's death reached Mekka, Abdullah had himself proclaimed Caliph by the inhabitants of the town and assumed the title of 'Amir Al Mnminin' (61 = 680-681 A.D.). The people of Medina having rebelled against the Ommayyads, Abdullah was proclaimed Caliph by the entire Hijaz. But the inhabitants of Medina were defeated by Muslim b. Okba at the battle of Al Harra (27th Dhul Hijja, 63 = 27th August 683) and Husain b. Numair who took Muslim's place in command of the army, proceeded to besiege Abdullah in Mekka. The siege, lasting for 64 days, had

14

in Medina, in Kufa, in Basra, and in Yaman the rule of the
Omayyads was renounced after the death of Yazid), but also in
Egypt and in Syria a portion of the inhabitants declared
for the son of Zubair. At their head stood the powerful
Dhahhak Ibn Kais* the former Governor of Damascus and
the Chief of Muawiya's body-guard.

To him flocked all the Arabs of the tribe of Kais for they
refused to take the oath of allegiance to Khalid whose mother
belonged the tribe of Kalb.† At Merj Rahit‡, some miles east

---

become very distressing for Abdullah when, having learned the death of Yazid,
Husain raised it. The greater portion of the Musulman Empire then joined
Abdullah, and he was at one swoop proclaimed Caliph in Iraq, Southern
Arabia and in a great part of Syria. He sent emissaries into Egypt, Palestine
and elsewhere to induce the inhabitants to recognise him as Caliph, and
everywhere appointed governors devoted to his cause. But Abdullah suffered a
blow in the defeat and death of Al Dhahhak al Fihri, one of the principal
agitators in his favour, at the battle of Marj Rahit, end of 64 or beginning of
65=684 A.D.). Having established his power Abdullah set to work to rebuild
the temple of the Kaba which had been partially destroyed at the time of the
siege of Mekka by Husain b. Numair. Meanwhile he began to oppress the
Kharijites. In the following year he caused Mohamed b. Al Hanafiyya with
all his family and seventeen notables of Kufa to be imprisoned near the
well of Zemzam. A serious injury to Abdullah's power was the defeat and
death of his brother Musab b. Al Zubair, his governor of Iraq (71=691).
Abdullah soon found his authority limited to Mekka alone, to which Hajjaj,
sent by Abdul Malik, laid siege on the 1st of Dhu-L-Ka'da 72 (25th March
692). The town and the temple were again bombarded but Abdullah kept
resolute for six and a half months, when his companions, even his two sons,
Hamza and Khubaib, being weary and at the end f their strength,
surrendered to Hajjaj. Abdullah, urged on by his mother, a woman of truly
Roman pride, returned to the field of battle and fought valiantly, till he was
slain. His body was fixed by Hajjaj to a gibbet at Al Hajun and after it was
hanging for sometime, it was, by Abdul Malik's orders, given back to his
mother Asma who buried it in the house of Safiya at Medina near the tombs of
the prophet, Abu Bakr and Omar. Ency. of Islam, Tr.]

* [See Muir's Caliphate pp. 328 et seq. Tr.; see Dozy, Ispanish Islam
pp. 73—74. Tr.]

† [See Zaydan, pp. 66-69. The bulk of the Yamenites became partisans
of Ali, excepting, however, those whom Moawiyyah conciliated with gifts, know-

of Damascus, they came to a battle which resulted in favour of Marwan. Without resting he reduced both the mutinous province of Syria and of Egypt. It was now easy for him to expel Musab,

---

ing that the favour of the Kuraish and his other adherents would not be sufficient. He therefore made overtures to the tribe of Kalb, and married one of their women, named Bahdal, who became the mother of his son Yazid. He easily obtained their help against the murderers of Othman, because Othman's wife was one of their tribe; but he also won them over with presents, so that they fought on his side. When he succeeded in his wars, and was firmly seated on the throne many tribes, both Mudarite and Yamenite, joined his party, and Kalb remained faithful to his son Yazid after his death, Yazid being their nephew on the mother's side.

When Yazid died Ibn al-Zubair remained in Meccah, as a claimant of the Caliphate; dissension arose among the Umayyads as to which they should choose—Khalid son of Yazid or Marwan Ibn al-Hakam, both of them Umayyads. Ibn Zubair had on his side the Kaisites (a division of Mudar); whereas the Kalbites of Yemen were on the side of Khalid, owing to his father's connection with them. Certain Umayyads then came forward and brought objections against Khalid on the score of youth, so the Umayyads agreed on Merwán, who was of mature years. Khalid, however, was to succeed him. Then came the battle of Marj Ráhit, between the followers of Ibn Zubair, and Marwán, respectively Kais and Kalb. Marwan won this battle, and so his Caliphate was secured. Then Marwan died without keeping his promise to Khalid, for he left the throne to his own son, 'Abd-al-Malik, a powerful ruler. Kalb continued to favour him, whereas Kais were against him, so throughout the Islamic Empire the Arabs were split into these two parties, called variously Kais and Kalb, Mudar and Yemenite, Nizár and Kahtan. The dissension between them spread through Syria, 'Irak, Egypt, Fars, Khorasan, Africa, Spain; everywhere the two factions were represented, and each got the upper hand alternately, with the changes in Caliphs, governors and lieutenants. The Mudarite governor would promote Mudarites, the Yeminite Yeminites. The balance was perpetually shifting. The distinction was of great importance in every branch of the administration, and even affected the appointment and dismissal of Caliphs, governors, etc., The preponderance of one of the parties at the time would often decide the appointment.

Kais, as we have seen, was against 'Abdul-Malik son of Marwan; still, they constituted the main support of his son Hisham, who favoured the Kaisites accordingly, and introduced their names into the register, i.e., assigned them permanent salaries and stipends. In his days the Kaisites were the dominant party, and the Mudarites as a whole became partisans of the Umayyads,

the brother of Abdullah Ibn Zubair, who had invaded Syria. He could even despatch troops to Medina to conquer afresh this important town, but his troops were driven back with losses.

---

especially after the death of Al-Walid Ibn Yazid whose mother was of the tribe Kais. Marwan Ibn Mohammad, last of the Umayyad Caliphs came forward to avenge his death, hoping to secure their support, in which he succeeded for the Mudarites supported him unswervingly till his death, whereas the Yeminites favoured the 'Abbasids when they rose.

Within these two main factions there was a variety of other factions that quarrelled and fought: notwithstanding this, the dignity of the Kuraish continued to be maintained and their influence to exceed that of all other tribes. When there was any danger of a province rebelling against its governor, a Kuraishite governor was ordinarily appointed, who would quickly succeed in restoring discipline.

The Kuraish were also divided, the chief division being that between the Umayyad and Hashimite families. Other Moslems would take up the cause of one or other of these families, whose rival claims led to much brawling; men would spend their time in urging their respective claims till the dispute assumed formidable proportions, and resulted in civil war and bloodshed. The Hashimites were powerful in the Hijaz and 'Irak, whereas the head quarters of the Umayyads were in Syria. The spheres of influence varied at different times. Sometimes the dispute began between rival poets, some of whom became celebrated for their performances in this field. The most famous poetic match of the sort was that between Sudaif, client of the Hashimites, and a fanatic adherant of the family, and Sayyas, an adherant of the Umayyads. These two poets used to go outside Meccah and satarise the rival families; the Meccans divided into two groups favouring the one or the other. Hence there were developed at Meccah two great parties, called Sudaifites and Sayyabites; they continued down to Abbasid days, when their names were changed into the 'embalmers' and the 'butchers.' Sudaif was the author of a poem recited before Al-Saffah, which caused the death of the Umayyad Sulaiman Ibn Hisham.

‡ [See Hurat, Hist. des. Arabes p. 264, Vol. I. Tr. "The Omayyads had however to pay dearly for this victory, for it destroyed the fundamental principle of the Arabian Empire (the victory at Merj Rahit in the beginning of 684). Hate once generated at Merj Rahit, the blood-feud there arising was so bitter that even the growing religious spirit of Islam was unable to make headway against it. The Arabs had previously been divided into numerous factions warring against each other, but now the battle of Merj

Ubaidullah and Husain won over Zufr Ibn Ha.ith and Sulaiman a
dazzling victory at Karkasiya*. Zufr was at one time Governor
of Kinesrin and was an ally of Dhahhak Ibn Kais, and had fled after
the battle at Merj Rahit towards the Euphrates. Sulaiman was a
Kharijite whom the rebels of Kufa chose as their chief after the
expulsion of the Omayyad governor. Even tbe son of Zubair was
jubilant over the defeat of Sulaiman. Abdullah† had hitherto
played in Mekka the modest rôle of "guardian of the temple"
and spoke more of the vices of the Omayyads than of his own
virtues, and strove to win the Kharijites over for his own
purposes. When he assumed, however, the title of the Caliph, a
breach was inevitable. The Kharijites remembered now that
Abdullah and his father Zubair had at first appeared against Ali
and had called for vengeance for the blood of Othman; while

Rahit created that intolerable race hatred between the Kais (the supporters
of Zubair) and Kalb tribes (the tribe which had long been resident in Syria
and with whom Muawiyya had became related by marriage, which spread to
other older racial opponents). The Kais were distributed throughout the
entire kingdom; the opposition towards them drove their opponents into the
ranks of the Kalb. The political parties became geneological branches
according to the theory of the Arabs, which regarded all political relationship
from an ethnical standpoint. And now for the first time, not in the remote
past, arose that opposition between the Northern and Southern Arabians which
permeated public life and which only in part coincided with actual racial
descent. Here it was the Kais, there the Kalb and under these party cries
the Arabs tore at each other henceforward throughout the whole empire, and
this purely political and particularist tribal feud undermined the rule of the
Arabs, au least as much as their religious political opposition to the authority
of the State itself which was thereby ruined; the governors could no longer
permanently hold aloof from the parties, and finally the Caliphs themselves
were unable to do so. Cambridge Medieval History, Vol II, p. 360. Tr.]

* [Some two hundred miles below Rakkah stand Karkasiya, the ancient
Circesium, on the left bank of the Tigris where the moiey of the Khabur river
flows in. Ibn Haukal describes it as a fine town surrounded by gardens but
Yaqut and Mustawfi both refer to it as a smaller place than the neighbouring
Rahbah. Lestrange p. 105 Tr.]

† [See, Snouck Hurgronje, Mekka Vol. I pp. 27 et seq, T.]

HISTORY OF THE ISLAMIC PEOPLES

they had declared the death of Othman as lawful, and had evinced the greatest attachment to the family of Ali. To avoid inconsistency and to use the unmerited death of Othman and the complicity of Ali, in the conspiracy as weapons against the descendants of Ali; Abdullah, when the Kharijites found fault with Othman, had to defend him, blaming those who, on account of a letter written, without his knowledge, had caused his murder.

Fortunately for Abdullah the Kharijites were split up into various sects. In Basra, where Nafi Ibn Azrak* was their chief, they showed greater firmness and determination, and desired forthwith to avenge the death of Husain and to take the field against all the enemies of the Alides. They even opposed the governor appointed by Abdullah Ibn Zubair, and to such an extent did they go in their opposition that the governor was compelled to drive them away by force of arms.

---

* [See Ibn Khallikan (note 3) Vol. II p. 514. "The heretical sect of the Azârika, or followers of Ibn-al-Azrak, a branch of the Kharijites, rejected equally the claims of Ali and Muawiya. Under the command of their chief and founder, Nâfi Ibn al-Azrak, they joined Abd Allah Ibn Az-Zubair at Mekka and fought in his defence, but, on discovering that he considered Othmân as a rightful Khalif, they abandoned his cause and proceeded to Basra in A. H. 64 (A.D. 683-4), where they took the oath of allegiance to Nâfi and established themselves at al-Ahwâz. The following year, their power increased considerably, and the people of Basra, who had incurred their enmity, obtained from Abd Allah Ibn Az-Zubair that a body of troops, under the order of Muslim Ibn Abîs, should march against them. The Azârika were repulsed from the territory of Basra and retreated to *Dulab* in the land of al-Ahwâz, where both parties encountered. The Azârika were here defeated with great loss, and Nâfi Ibn al-Azrak fell in the battle, which was also fatal to Muslim Ibn Abîs. As the insurgents still continued to be dangerous, Muhallah Ibn Abi Sufra, an able general, marched against them by order of Abd Allah Ibn al-Harith, Governor of Basra. Their final subjugation was not effected till about A. H. 70 (A. D. 689).—[Abu l-Mahâsin's al-Bahr az-Zâkhir. El-Makin's Historia Saracenica, p. 60. See also Price's Retrospect, Vol. 1. pages 429, 440 and 446. For their political and religious doctrines, See Dr. Cureton's Shatrastâni, page. 98.

In Kufa on the other hand Sulaiman waited for a favourable opportunity and he therefore maintained friendly relations with the governor of Abdullah. Sulaiman, however, was soon shaken out of his easy, comfortable position by Mukhtar who, ambitious to a degree, like most of the leading men of the time, cloaked his selfishness under the garb of piety and specious declamations. He travelled to Mekka to invite Husain to place himself at the head of the Kufans. After the death of Husain he was put into prison, but at the instance of his brother-in-law, Abdullah Ibn Omar, he was released; whereupon he repaired to Mekka to the son of Zubair. Abdullah Ibn Zubair got round Mukhtar by all manner of gifts and promises and humoured him so long as he stood in need of his help. But after Arabia, Egypt and Iraq had done homage to him he thought that he no longer needed the services of Mukhtar. He therefore neglected him and refused him the governorship of Iraq because he feared his guile and ambition.

Mukhtar took now another route to power and riches—the goal of his ambition. He travelled to Kufa, effected a junction with the Kharijites, and asserted that he was sent to them by Mohamed Ibn Hanafiya,* a surviving son of Ali in Mekka, whose mother came from the tribe of Hanafiyya, to lead them against the murderers of Husain; since Sulaiman was apparently neglecting the performance of this duty. Mukhtar was, however, arrested by the governor of Abdullah. To Sulaiman therefore no alternative was left, if he was to retain the confidence of the Kharijites, but to march, according to their desire, against the Syrians, under the command of Ubaidullah. When Sulaiman reached Karkasiya with some 8,000 men; Zufr who held this fortified town for Abdullah Ibn Zubair, caused the gates to be shut, partly out of fear of the rabble which had joined these fanatics, and partly because he knew that the Kharijites hated Abdullah no less than they did the Omayyads;

---

* [Ibn Khallikan, Vol. II. p. 574. Tr.]

still he requested Sulaiman to remain encamped in the neighbourhood of the town to co-operate with him in its defence against the
advancing Syrians and to seek shelter in case of defeat within
its walls. But Sulaiman, paying no attention to his advice,
and pressed onward by the war-loving fanatics, continued his
march until he met the enemy at Ainwardah between Karkasiya
and Rakka. The vanguard of the Syrians, taken by
surprise, was cut to pieces, but the main portion of the army,
under Husain Ibn Numair, reinforced by Ubaidullah (the
Kharijite force becoming in the meantime thinner and thinner)
won on the third day of the battle, a complete victory over
Sulaiman who perished on the battle field. This battle took place
shortly before the death of Merwan who, failing to keep his
promise, was murdered by his wife in April, 685. To satisfy the
party of the legitimate heir to the throne—Khalid Ibn Yazid,
he had married his mother, promising her that he would nominate her son as his successor, but when he found himself
sufficiently strong to disregard the supporters of Khalid he
nominated his own son Abdul Malik, to the detriment of
Khalid. When Abdul Malik ascended the throne he was in
a far worse position than was Muawiya the first on his
accession. He had, like Muawiya, not only Persia, Iraq and
Arabia against him, but even in Syria itself he found opposition
from the supporters of Khalid on the one hand and those of
Abdullah Ibn Zubair on the other *. The followers of
Abdullah had suffered a severe defeat at Merj Rahit † but
their wrath against the Omayyads grew more and more ; it
being further embittered by the fact of the influence of the
Yamanides, on whom the Omayyad government mainly relied.
But greater than at the time of Ali, to be sure, was the disunion

---

* [Khalid whom he had supplanted. See, Wellhausen, Das Arabische
Reich und sein Sturz, p. 115 Tr.]

† [Merwan was opposed by Ibn Zubair's party. This battle was fought
between the party of Merwan on the one hand and the party of Zubair, headed
by Dhahhak and supported by the Bani Kais and the northern t.ibes on the
other. Merwan won. Tr.]

among the opponents of the Omayyads; for as already mentioned the Kharijites had renounced the son of Zubair and were now inclined to recognise Mohamed Ibn Al-Hanafiyya as their Imam. Thus the Kharijites and the Zubarites now fought with one another for the throne. Basra was the first theatre of the bloody encounter between the combatants. The Governor of Zubair, installing himself by force of arms, had to drive out of the town the Kharijites called Azrakites, after their leader, Nafi Ibn Azrak who, with the help of the newly enlisted troops, took possession of the town for the second time. But when Abdullah sent Muslim Ibn Ubayy with a small army he was driven out once again and was killed in the flight to Ahwas. The Azrakites thereupon appointed another leader and made the entire country between Ahwas and Basra thoroughly unsafe; killing every one not belonging to their party. They would probably have occupied Basra once again if Muhallab, the Governor of Khorasan, had not routed and forced them to fly into the interior of Persia. But scarcely were the Azrakites conquered when Abdullah was again threatened by the Kaisanides *i.e.* by the followers of Mukhtar, called also Kaisan. Mukhtar once more out of regard for Abdullah Ibn Omar, had been released from prison. On his release he swore that he would not take part in any movement against Abdullah Ibn Yazid, the then governor of Kufa. Mukhtar kept to his word so long as Abdullah Ibn Yazid was in office, but when a new Governor came to Kufa he began intrigues afresh, and with the help of Ibrahim, the son of Malik-ul-Ashtar, who had fought so bravely for Ali, took possession of the town as well as the fort, to which the governor had fled. Mukhtar acted with magnanimity towards the fugitive governor and even against his enemies in the town.* He only proceeded with rigour when they, while his troops were marching against Ubaidullah, rose in arms against him. The troops

* [*Kufa. Tr.]

113

were recalled as quickly as possible to chastise the rebels; and to gratify the fanatical *Shiites* Mukhtar put to the sword all those who had fought against Husain at Karbala. When Kuĺa was swept clean of his enemies Mukhtar again sent Ibrahim against Ubaidullah. On the bank of the river Zab in the neighbourhood of Mosul* the two contending armies met face to face (August, 686). The Syrians were far superior to the Iraqians in number, but the personal heroism of Ibrahim, the overflowing

---

* [Mosul (Al-Mawasil), the chief city of Diyar Rabîah, stands on the Western bank of the Tigris at the point where a series of loops in the river coalesce to form a single main stream, and Al-Mawasil, meaning 'the confluence,' is said to take its name from this fact. In Sassanian times the city which existed here was called Bûdh Ardashîr. Under the Omayyads Mosul rose to importance, a bridge of boats was set across the Tigris, connecting the city on the western side with the ruins of Nineveh on the east bank, and Mosul became the capital of the Jazirah province under Marwân II, the last of the Omayyad Caliphs, who also built here what afterwards came to be known as the old Mosque.

Ibn Hawkal who was at Mosul in 358 (969) describes it as a fine town with excellent markets, surrounded by fertile districts of which the most celebrated was that round Nînaway (Nineveh) where the Prophet Yûnis (Jonah) was buried. In the 4th (10th) century the population consisted chiefly of Kurds, and the numerous districts round Mosul, occupying all Diyâr Rabî'ah, are carefully enumerated by Ibn Hawkal. Mukaddasî praises the numerous excellent hostelries of Mosul, and the town, he says, was extraordinarily well built, being in plan a semi-circle, and about a third the size of Baṣrah. Its castle was named Al-Murabha'ah (the Square) and it stood on the affluent called the Nahr Zubaydah; within its precincts was held the Wednesday Market (Sûk-al-Arba'â) by which name also the Castle was sometimes known The Friday Mosque (that of Marwân II) stood a bowshot from the Tigris, on a height to which steps led up. The roof of this building was vaulted in stone, and it had no doors to close the doorways going from the main building of the Mosque into its court. The market streets of Mosul were for the most part roofed over, eight of the chief thoroughfares are named by Mukaddasî, and the houses of the town stretched for a considerable distance along the Tigris bank. Mukaddasi adds that formerly Mosul had borne the name of Khawlân: and that the Kaṣr-al-Khalifah, 'the palace of the Caliph,' stood on the opposite bank of the river, half a league from the town, overlooking Nineveh. This palace of old had been protected by strong ramparts, which the winds had

enthusiasm of his troops, with whom Mukhtar had sent a chest with all manner of relics of Ali and Husain, as also the treason of a Syrian general who belonged to the beaten party of Dhahhak Ibn Kais, and who wanted on this occasion to wreak vengeance on Ubaidullah and the Yamanide tribes, decided the battle in favour of Mukhtar, who in the very same castle received the head of Ubaidullah where some six years before Ubaidullah had gloated over the head of Husain.

Thus was Husain avenged.

After this victory Mukhtar once more entered into negotiations with the son of Zubair, and hoped to obtain from him after all the much coveted governorship of Kufa but the whole scheme miscarried on account of their deep-rooted mutual distrust. When Mukhtar, however, sent some thousand men to Arabia ostensibly to defend Medina in concert with the Zubairides against a Syrian army but really to secure this town for himself; they were surrounded and massacred by the troops of Abdullah. Only in one quarter alone could Mukhtar now look for support, and that was with the son of Ali. But, weak and vacillating, he would not formally acknowledge

---

overthrown, and the ruins, through which flowed the stream called the Nahr-al-Khawsar, were when Mukaddasi wrote occupied by fields.

In the year 580 (1184) Mosul was visited and described by Ibn Jubayr. Shortly before this date the famous Nur-ad-Din, under whose banner Saladin began his career, had built the new Friday Mosque in the market place, but the old mosque of Marwan II still stood on the river bank, with its beautifully ornamented oratory and iron window-gratings. In the upper town was the great fortress, and the town walls with towers at intervals extended down to and along the river banks, a broad street connecting upper with lower Mosul. Beyond the walls were extensive suburbs with many small Mosques, hostelries and bath houses. The Maristân (or hospital) was famous, also the great market buildings called Kayṣarîyah, and there were also numerous colleges here. Kazwini gives a list of the various Dayars or Christian convents which were found in the vicinity of Mosul, and he notes especially the deep ditch and high walls of the Mosul fortress. All round the town were numerous gardens, irrigated, he says, by waterwheels. Le Strange, pp. 87-89. Tr.]

him as his representative in Iraq. But when for persistent refusal to do him homage Abdullah caused his arrest, and when he saw that none but Mukhtar could effect his release, then alone did he decide to address him in a letter as his Caliph (representative). Armed with this letter and crowned with success in obtaning the liberation of Mohamed, Mukhtar rose in the estimation of the Kharijites. But his position in Kufa was not free from serious difficulties inasmuch as the majority of the inhabitants were other than the] Kharijites. Hostile to him these were in alliance with the refugees who, after the unsuccessful insurrection at Kufa, had emigrated to Basra where Musab, brother of Abdullah, ruled as governor. Distrustful of the co-operation of the fickle Kufans Musab could not take the field against Mukhtar until he was assisted by the brave Muhallab who had joined him from Persia, and until his army actually outnumbered that of Mukhtar. The battle which was fought (April, 687) at Harura in the neighbourhood of Kufa lasted the whole day. Only towards the evening did the beaten army of Mukhtar withdraw into the town and he himself with some thousand men flung himself into the fort, hoping that his supporters outside and especially his governor Ibrahim would hasten to his relief. But when several days had passed away without any relief having come and when want of provisions had become acute and poignant; for Musab had surrounded the fort, then, did Mukhtar call upon the garrison to follow him in the attack upon the besiegers asking them to die rather with sword in hand than perish of hunger or on the surrender of the fort be slaughtered like sheep. But only nineteen responded to his call and died as heroes by his side. The troops that had remained behind in the fort were grievously deceived in their expectations. At the instance of Musab, as Mukhtar had prophesied, they were mowed down without mercy or compassion.

So long as his enemies fought among themselves the Caliph Abdul Malik used his own troops for the defence of the northern provinces which where threatened alike by the Greeks and the Mardites. But when after the fall of Mukhtar even Ibrahim, the governor of Mosul, went over to Musab, and the supporters of Ali were either killed or driven away to the extreme East of Persia, and the whole of Arabia, Iraq and Persia lay at the feet of Abdullah, to Abdul Malik no other option was left, if he were to save Syria, but to gird up his loins for a battle with Abdullah. He had therefore to make peace with the Byzantines (689). But while Abdul Malik was on his way to Mesopotamia an insurrection broke out at Damascus, headed by his cousin Amr Ibn Said, who had won his spurs under Merwan in the war against the Zubairites and to whom Merwan is said to have even promised the throne. The Caliph had therefore to return to Damascus to suppress the rebellion. This was all the easier for him to do as the people of Damascus would neither fight Abdul Malik nor were they prepared to expose themselves to a siege. Amr had to surrender the town and accept the amnesty which the Caliph offered to him. Relying on no oath and wishing to leave no enemy behind, Abdul Malik violated the promise made to Amr. Before his second expedition Amr was caused to be executed or according to some reports the Caliph himself killed him. After the death of Amr and some other leaders of the conspiracy Abdul Malik, without any further danger, could safely lead an expedition to Iraq. He himself reduced several towns on the Upper Euphrates to subjection; while Khalid Ibn Abdullah, in the absence of Musab, tried to take possession of Basra which sheltered within its walls not a few of the tribesmen of the Arabs, domiciled in Syria and who were only too eager to welcome the Omayyads.

Mighty as was the effort of Mohamed to weld all the Arabs into one great nation; yet in this direction he failed lamentably, for the tribal bond proved stronger and more enduring than any other tie, religious or political.* When the

* [See, Dozy, Spanish Islam pp. 24 et sqq. Tr.]

Governor of Abdullah received reinforcement from Kufa and when Musab himself hastened thither Khalid had again to withdraw. Musab, however, could not but proceed, ·vith the utmost vigour, against all suspected of treasonable communication with the enemy; and left a strong garrison behind, in charge of one of his most trusted officers—a step which the steady advance of the Caliph made so necessary for the defence of Iraq. The insurrection at Basra told heavily against Musab. The people in Kufa lost all confidence in him, since they knew that several of his generals were in disloyal correspondence with his opponent. There was not much left for the whole of Iraq to pass without a blow into the hands of Abdul Malik. Possibly the fear of the severe Government of the Syrians alone still induced the Kufans to follow Musab. When Musab gave battle to the Caliph in the neighbourhood of Muskan, on one of the arms of the Tigris, the battle remained undecisive so long as Ibrahim was in command. But after his death it degenerated into a shameful flight. Musab himself would not, even when he saw himself forsaken, surrender to the mercy of Abdul Malik. "A man like myself" said he, "should either leave the battle-field as a conqueror or be borne away as a corpse." Even his son Isa, whom he begged to go away to Mekka to his brother, held out with him for "the women of Quraish were not to slander him after his death and speak of him as one who had forsaken his father." Thus the two, father and son, fought until they succumbed to the blows of the Syrians (Nov., 690). Abdul Malik, without any further resistance, now triumphantly entered Kufa where he also received the homage of the town of Basra. The news of the death of Musab had already secured the ascendency there for the party of the Omayyads. Even Persia bowed to the yoke of the Syrians when Muhallab went over to the victorious party and made his troops take the oath of allegiance to Abdul Malik. The Caliph now directed his undivided attention to Abdullah who of late had fallen into an inconceivable lethargy but who on account of his residence at Mekka, the birth place of the Prophet, the very spiritual centre of Islam, and by the influence which he exerted on the pilgrims assembling there, year by year, yet remained a dangerous rival to consider and to reckon with. From Iraq he sent Hajjaj Ibn Yusuf to Mekka (Oct, 691) who was not long in being convinced that he could advance without opposition as far as the holy territory and that he could even undertake to besiege Mekka as soon as the Caliph sent him the necessary reinforcements.

True, by his sermons and speeches, Abdullah had won, great applause—but they were little calculated to inspire enthusiasm in the Arabs (intent upon worldly gain, power, glory and riches) to take up arms for him, since not only was his character unlovely and unlovable but his despicable greed was an abomination to many.

Moreover the natural intelligence of the Arabs was not slow in discovering the real motive for his venomous vituperations against the Omayyads. They clearly saw that he would, as soon as opportunity arose, justify his claims to the Caliphate by all manner of arguments.

If they were, in the existing citcumstances, to waive their right to elect a new Caliph—they would have on the one hand the Omayyads, as avengers and successors of Othman and on the other the descendants of Ali. Therefore not only the Kharijites but also pious, simple Muslims would set Abdullah down as a usurper. He boasted indeed of his close kinship with Khadija and Ayesha, wives of Mohamed; with Asma, the daughter of Abu Bakr, who was his mother; and with Safiya, the aunt of the Prophet, who was his grand-mother; but, with justice Abdullah Ibn Abbas replied to him that all these good ladies were only ennobled by the Prophet of God and therefore he could not rank higher than those who constituted members of his family.

At the request of Hajjaj, Abdul Malik sent from Syria to

119

Mekka some thousand men under Tarik Ibn Amr—the very same Tarik who also reduced Medina to subjection. Several attacks of the Mekkans were repelled; the town was surrounded and cut off from all provisions; while the ballistas created considerable havoc. This state of affairs lasted well-nigh a year until the Mekkans marched out, in troops, and begged for the mercy of Hajjaj.

Now nothing was left for Abdullah (even his two sons went over to the enemy) but either to surrender or die with sword in hand as the defender of the holy temple. He, personally, perhaps, would have preferred the former course, but his heroic mother persuaded him to close his life of doubtful virtue with at least a glorious death.

My son, she spoke, thou alone knowest thy mind. If thou art convinced of the truth of thy cause and hast summoned the people to defend only truth and righteousness; then, persist in thy path and expose not thy name to the scorn and contempt of the sons of Omayya. If, on the contrary, thou hast only pandered to thy ambition, thou art a wicked servant of God and thou hast hurled thyself and thy followers to ruin. But if thou sayest: Truth and right were indeed with me, but when my companions became weak, I lost courage. To this I reply: This is not the conduct of free men with whom, all supreme and all paramount, ever remains a sense of righteousness. How long hast thou still to live in this world? Better, thou shouldst die at the hand of thy enemy.*

Abdullah, who in his youth had given numerous proofs of his courage and heroism, was nerved again by these words, and soon came back to his mother, with helmet and coat-of-mail, to wish her farewell. When embracing him, she felt the coat-of-mail beneath his garment, and said: he who seeks death in battle, needs no coat-of-mail. He then took it off, repaired to his few

---

* [Compare, Wüstenfeld's Die chroniken der Stadt Mekka p. 142. Tr.]

companions, who wanted to share his fate with him, and requested them to take off their helmets, to enable him, once again, to see their loyal faces. When this was done, he said : " Take care more of your sword than of your eyes ; for a man without sword is feebler than a woman ." Then, with a small band of his loyal friends, he met the Syrians advancing towards the Temple, and fought until, struck by a stone on the forehead, he fell lifeless (1st October, 692).

The whole of Arabia now acknowledged the sovereignty of Abdul Malik. And Hajjaj, who remained behind as governor of of Mekka and Medina, took care that no fresh revolutionary tendencies asserted themselves. Iraq and Egypt were administered by the two brothers of the Caliph, Bishr and Abdul Aziz ; the opposition in Khorasan was crushed by Waki Ibn Amr, the prefect of Merv ; while Muhallab kept Persia in check, where the Kharijites, in spite of repeated defeats, rose ever and anon under new leaders. After the death of Bishr, when the Iraqians, who took the field with Muhallab against the Kharijites, left the camp and returned to their home, Hajjaj was appointed governor of Iraq ; the very same Hajjaj, who had already proved in Arabia how well he understood the method of bringing the rebels to obedience. His bold and fearless *début* in the midst of a refractory population and the terrible threats which he uttered against disobedience produced the desired effect upon the cowardly Kufans. Thus when he swore at the end of his speech that every one who had left the camp of Muhallab should within three days return to him and place himself under his banner on pain of death ; only one man remained behind, whom he caused to be executed, although he protested that he had sent his son instead of going himself to the army. With equally unrelenting severity did Hajjaj act in Basra until he had compelled the deserters to leave the town.

Thus Muhallab was again in a position to prosecute with vigour the war against the Kharijites. But while Muhallab was

121

16

fighting the Azrakites in Persia, who after their expulsion from Khuzistan maintained themselves for a long time under Katari in Faristan and Kirman ; other fanatics under Saleh, Shabib, and Mutarrif, roamed about in other provinces, preaching insurrection against the Omayyads, or calling for a new election of the Caliph, or trying to take possession of the Caliphate themselves. They condemned Othman and Ali alike ; the former because he deviated from the precepts of his predecessors and promoted the godless to the highest offices of the state ; the latter because he set up men as arbitrators over things divine, and allowed himself to be surrounded by infamous creatures. Saleh was killed at Khanikin but Shabib held out longer, because he maintained discipline, found sympathy and impressed people by his piety. Eluding their grasp he would deliver sudden attacks upon the hostile troops. He was now in the neighbourhood of Madain, now on the southern borders of Adherbaijan, now in Kirman ; then all of a sudden he would make his appearance again in the neighbourhood of Mosul or on the frontier of Syria. He even twice attacked the town of Kufa. During the second attack, only after three days fighting and after the Syrian troops had arrived, did Hajjaj manage to drive him out of the town. In the year 697 after a portion of his people had been bribed by Hajjaj ; to escape the traitors he wanted to cross the river Karun, but while doing so he met his death. Mutarrif was a follower of Shabib, but he differed from him in this that while he would limit the Caliphate to the family of the Prophet, Shabib, who himself aspired to soverignty, maintained that the most distinguished of the faithful should be elected regardless of family connection; for he stood nearest to the Prophet who carried out his precepts with the greatest diligence. Mutarrif was the prefect of Madain and he had hoped that the prefects of Hulwan and Hamadan would make common cause with him. When he found himself deceived in his expectations, he had already gone much too far to retrace his foot-steps. He knew that he had incurred the wrath of Hajjaj and he knew that vengeance would be sure and swift. He yet roamed about in Northern Persia, pursued by the prefects of Rayy and Isphahan, and this went on and on until, as with many an another fanatic before him, there was no other alternative left but to die sword in hand.

More dangerous than these rebels, who were feared more on account of their fanaticism and their seditious speeches than on account of their strength and power, was Abdur Rahman, the son of Mohamed lbn Asghath*. He was Governor of Sijistan and

---

* [Abdur Rahman B. Mohamed B. Al Ashath, a Kindite general who revolted against Hajjaj. Being descended from the old kings of Kinda, Abdur Rahman was at first the recipient of much kindness from Hajjaj who went so far as to marry his son Mohamed to Abdur Rahman's sister. In 76 (695=6) Hajjaj sent him with an army to defend Mada'in against Shabib. In 80 (699) after the defeat of Ubaidullah b. Abi Bakr by Rutbil, king of Kabulistan, Hajjaj gave Abdur Rahman the lieutenancy of Sijistan and the command of an army magnificently equipped to make war against Rutbil. Abdur Rahman's campaigns were replete with successes, but Hajjaj nevertheless sent him rough letters blaming his conduct.

Urged by his soldiers he openly revolted and declared war against Al Hajjaj (81=700). Before setting out for Iraq Abdur Rahman concluded a treaty of alliance with Rutbil, who pledged himself to help him in case of need and to afford him a place of refuge in his country. In the beginning Abdur Rahman was victorious, but at the battle of Al Zawiya, his army was routed. He fled to Kufa, where the Caliph Abdul Malik sent his son Abdullah and his brother Mohamed to negotiate with him, even proposing the recall of Al Hajjaj. Abdur Rahman did not accept the offers of the Caliph and thus declared himself as his enemy. The battle of Dair al-Djamajam (shaban 82—September 701,) was disastrous for Abdur Rahman and that of Maskin completed his downfall. He fled towards Sijistan and on his arrival at Bust the prefect Iyad b. Himyan, loaded him with chains, intending to give him up to Al Hajjaj. But Rutbil, true to his promise, came to free him and took him to his own country. Once more, however, at the instigation of his army Abdur Rahman returned to Bust to try his luck against Al Hajjaj but he soon returned to Rutbil. Finally Rutbil himself, yielding to the promises and

had received from Hajjaj, who in a way was the viceroy of all the eastern provinces of the Empire, the chief command of an army intended for an expedition against the Prince of Kabul. Already his predecessor had waged war against this prince but he did so unsuccessfully because having penetrated too far into the interior he was surrounded suddenly by the hostile troops. To avoid a similar fate Abdur Rahman proceeded with the utmost caution. While advancing he left behind small garrisons in secure places to keep himself constantly in communication with Sijistan. When he had penetrated well into Kabulistan he took the homeward journey—postponing further conquests till the following year. Hajjaj accused him of weakness and cowardice and commanded him either to proceed onward or to surrender his command to another. When Abdur Rahman communicated this message to his generals they grew angry, denounced Hajjaj, paid homage to Abdur Rahman as their *Amir* and without actually shaking off their allegiance to the Caliph they summoned Ibn Ashath to march against Hajjaj. Thereupon Abdur Rahman concluded peace with the Prince of Kabul and strove to win Muhallab, the then governor of Khorasan, over to his side. Muhallab, tried to bring him back to obedience, but when he failed, he informed Hajjaj of the threatening danger and counselled him to defer his attack upon Abdur Rahman until the Iraqians had returned to their homes. Hajjaj did not accept this advice and considered it dangerous to throw open to rebels towns like Kufa and Basra. He therefore with his troops advanced towards Shuster, and awaited Abdur Rahman on the banks of the river Karun, but, as Muhallab had foreseen, the Iraqians, anxious to get home,

---

specially to the threats of Hajjaj, gave Abdur Rahman up to the emissary of the latter. When Abdur Rahman reached Al Rukhadj he threw himself from the top of the tower and was killed (85 = 704 A.D.). Houtsma's Encyc. of Islam. See Dozy's Spanish Islam. pp. 37 et seq. Tr.]

fought with unusual vigour and courage and forced the Syrians
to retire to Basra. Here a second battle, and a murderous one,
was fought. Immense was the loss on both sides, still Hajjaj
succeeded in holding out at Basra ; while Abdur Rahman wended
his way to Kufa where, with the assistance of the population
favourably disposed towards him, he succeeded in taking possession
of the fort. After the loss of Kufa, Hajjaj found himself
constrained to evacuate even Basra, because he was cut off from
communication with Syria and had therefore to retire to the
neighbourhood of Ain Tamar. Ever since his attack upon Iraq,
Abdur Rahman declared war not only against Hajjaj but, assum-
ing the rôle of Prince of the Faithful, took the field against
the Caliph as well. His troops grew more and more in number.
Thus, by the time he advanced against the Caliph he reckoned
100,000 under his banner. In spite of the advice of Hajjaj, who
reminded the Caliph of the consequences of Othman's weakness
and pointed out that iron could only be forged with iron, the Caliph
entered into negotiations with Abdur Rahman. He not only
promised complete forgiveness to the Iraqians but also assured
them of equal privileges with the Syrians in matters of pay
and pension. To Abdur Rahman he was prepared even to allow
a governorship of his own choice for life, and to appoint in the
place of Hajjaj a brother of the Caliph as governor of Iraq.
Abdur Rahman was inclined to accept these terms but his troops,
believing themselves, unconquerable, renounced afresh their
allegiance to the Caliph. Such being the position of affairs,
the Caliph was once more forced to appeal to the sword
of Hajjaj. For several months the two armies lay face to face
in their well protected camps. In July 702 A. D., however,
they came to a battle which ended in a victory for Hajjaj.
According to some reports, betrayed by the commander of his left
wing, Abdur Rahman fled to Kufa but as the larger portion of
his army had been disbanded and the Syrians were on his track,
he could not maintain himself there. He had to abandon the

town to the vengeance of Hajjaj. Abdur Rahman tried once again the fortune of war at Maskan where many readers of the Qur'an stood by his side and fought for him with absolute contempt of death. When unsuccessful here too, he fled to Bost. Here he was arrested and was about to be made over to the Caliph when he was rescued by the Prince of Kabul. He now placed himself at the head of the numerous malcontents in Sijistan but neither here nor in Khorasan could he secure a footing and was finally compelled to fly to Kabul where he ended his days. According to some reports he died a natural death, according to others the Prince of Kabul, threatened with a war by the Caliph, thought of surrendering him. He therefore committed suicide.

The insurrection of Abdur Rahman, and the fickleness of Kufa and Basra, brought once more to light, led to the foundation of Wasit, situated midway, whose garrison was to hold these two mutinous towns in check. The troubles at home under the Caliph Abdul Malik stood in the way of any great extension of the Empire abroad; still the Islamic Empire achieved many heroic feats of arms and acquired in various directions not inconsiderable enlargements.

After the subjection of the Slavs the Emperor Justinian II rescinded the peace.* Mohamed, the brother of the Caliph, who commanded the Arab troops, inflicted with the help of the Slav auxiliaries whom he bribed, a tremendous defeat upon the Greeks at Sebastapolis (693);† while another Arab general drove

---

* [Muawiya made a treaty with the Emperor Constantine IV (Its terms see Bury, Vol. II. p. 312.). In 685 Abdul Malik, to maintain peace with the empire, renewed the treaty with slightly altered conditions (page 314). Abdul Malik, renewed with Justinian II the peace which he had concluded with Constantine (page 320). This peace Justinian II dissolved. In 692 be refused to receive a new Saracen coinage introduced by Abdul Malik, inscribed with verses of the Qur'an. This led to the battle which took place in Cilicia, near Sebastapolis. Tr.]

† [(De Goeje fixes 692 as the date of the battle of Sebastapolis.)]

them out of Southern Armenia. In the following year, however, these advantages slipped out of the hands of the Arabs and they concluded once more a humiliating peace, but when this peace was broken by Justinian because he declined to receive the Muslim coinage, containing inscriptions which offended his religious susceptibilities, the Arabs, by a dazzling victory, wiped completely out the disgrace of several years of demoralising submission and re-occupied the provinces of Cilicia and Armenia.

Now every year greater or smaller fights took place with varying results. Predatory expeditions against the enemies' country were regularly and continually undertaken. The Arabs would now advance as far as Erzrum, and then again would traverse northern Syria as far as Antioch, plundering and murdering the Greeks.

In Africa Hasan Ibn Numan fought the Byzantines and re-conquered the whole of the Northern Coast as far as Carthage. But when he penetrated into the interior he was beaten back and was compelled by the Berbers, who were led by a priestess, to withdraw to Barka. This priestess, however, was secretly murdered and Hasan, once again, marched as a conquerer over the whole of the province of Kairowan.*

But while he had gone to Syria to celebrate his triumphal entry, the Emperor Leontius sent the Patrician John with a fleet to Africa, who re-conquered Carthage and drove the Arabs back to Barka. But since Hasan could not agree with the Governor of Egypt and died shortly after, Musa, the son of Nusair, was sent to Africa with fresh troops (697-98). He drove the Greeks for ever from Carthage and gradually succeeded in

---

* [Almost due south of Carthage the city of Kairowan was founded in the reign of Constantine IV by Okba (670); sixt years later it was taken by the Christians, then retaken by the Saracens, and taken yet again by the Christians (683), in whose power it remained until it was recovered by Hasan, whom Abdul Malik sent against Africa at the head of a large army (697).

**

conquering the whole of Africa right up to the Atlantic. Even in Transoxiana the frontier of Islam was extended by Muhallab, and after him by his son Yazid who succeeded him as Governor of Khorasan.*

Only by a year did the Caliph survive the terrible insurrection of Abdul Rahaman. He died, after a reign of one and twenty years, at the age of about 60 (October 8th, 705). His brother Abdul Aziz, Governor of Egypt, died two years earlier. Towards the end of Abdul Aziz's life there was a misunderstanding, nay, a serious quarrel, between them because according to the will of their father, Abdul Aziz was to succeed to the Caliphate ; while Abdul Malik was anxious to appoint his sons Walid and Sulaiman as his successors. It is even suggested that Abdul Aziz was poisoned at the instance of the Caliph and was thus got rid of. After the death of Abdul Aziz the arrangement made by the Caliph met with no further opposition ; although there were individuals—pious men—who sought to avoid the oath of allegiance on the ground that the taking of the oath of allegiance to another in the life-time of the reigning Caliph, was opposed to the principles of Islam. Such fanatics, therefore, as in their opposition were actuated by no

Hasan also conquered Carthage and compelled it to receive a garrison. But before the year was over Leontius sent an efficient general, John the Patrician, in command of the entire Roman fleet, to rescue Africa from the invader. When John reached Carthage he found that the Saracens had secured the entrance to the port by a strong chain. But, bursting through this obstacle, he expelled the garrison from the city ; and then freed all the other fortified towns from their Saracen occupants. Thus in a short space of time the Roman dominion was re-established, and the successful general wintered at Carthage, waiting for Imperial behests from Constantinople. In the meantime Abdul Malik prepared a larger fleet than he had sent to the Western Seas before, and early in 698 his armament arrived at Carthage and drove the Roman vessels from the harbour. Seeing that with his present forces he had no reasonable prospect of holding out against a Saracen siege, John returned to the East in order to obtain reinforcements. Bury, Vol. II, pp. 353-4 Tr.].

*[See, Ibn Khallikan, Vol. III, pp. 508 et sqq. Tr.]

motives, he let go unpunished. Indeed, throughout the whole
course of his reign he uniformly acted with mercy and
generosity unless forced to take a different course by reasons
of State. Further he was always for peace; peace at home
and peace abroad, and not until reduced to an absolute necessity
would he have recourse to arms. He had passed through
bitter experiences in life. He was only 10 when Othman
was murdered and his father Merwan saved, with the greatest
difficulty, from the clutches of death. The dangers, which he
personally faced or passed through at various stages of his life,
reminded him of the fickleness of fortune and the transitoriness
of things earthly, and turned his vision to the life beyond the
grave. He lived according to the precepts of the Qur'an without
wearing the cloak of hypocrisy. He always kept the middle course
between extravagance and stinginess. Only towards the famous
poets of his time was his generosity unbounded.* Even the
christian poet Akhtal found a friendly reception in his court
and filled a distinguished position in his palace.†

Being the governor of Hajr in his youth he had come to
know personally the working of the Government offices; he
therefore as Caliph effected many improvements, among them
the substitution of Arabic in the place of Persian in all
branches of the administration.‡

---

* [Abdul Malik, as patron of letters, see Weil's Gesch. d. Ch. Vol. I pp.
485 et sqq. Tr.]

† [See, Jarrett's translation of Suyuti p. 226 note Tr.]

‡ [Abdul Malik, says De Goeje, reconstituted the administration of the
Empire on Arabic principles. Up to the year 63 the Muslims had no special
coinage of their own, and chiefly used Byzantine and Persian money, either
imported or struck by themselves. Muawiya, indeed, had struck *Dinars* and
Dirhams with a muslim inscription, but his subjects would not accept them as
there was no cross upon them. Abdul Malik instituted a purely Islamic
coinage. If we may believe Theophanes, who says that Justinian II refused
to receive these coins in payment of the tribute, and therefore declared the

Finding the whole of the Empire free from the pretenders and clear of rebellion, Walid, on his accession, was able to devote his whole-hearted attention to the improvement of the affairs at home : the amelioration of agriculture, the growth of prosperity, the establishment of charitable institutions, the diffusion of learning and notably the extension of the Caliphate. Throughout the length and breadth of the Empire *mosques* were built, schools established, streets laid out, fountains dug, alms-houses and hospitals founded. Nor were the blind, the lame and persons otherwise disabled, neglected or forgotten. They also were provided with homes. By unrelenting severity on the one hand and extreme solicitude for the public weal on the other ; Walid managed to hold together an Empire which stretched from Kashgar and Multan to the Atlantic Sea. In the first year of his Caliphate he tried, by a mild and beneficent policy, to win Arabia over to him and with that object in view he appointed his pious cousin (later on Caliph Omar II), son of Abdul Aziz, governor of Medina, Under Walid, Iraq and Persia remained as before under Hajjaj who maintained peace by means of terror and threat. Moved by political considerations Hajjaj recommended to the Caliph the dismissal of Omar from the governorship of Medina ;

---

treaty at an end, we must put the beginning of the coinage at least two years earlier. Hajjaj coined silver *Dirhams* at Kufa in 604. A still greater innovation was that Arabic became the official language of the State. In the conquered countries till then, not only had the Greek and Persian administration been preserved, but Greek remained the official language in the Western, Persian in the Eastern Provinces. All officials were now compelled to know Arabic and to conduct their administration in that language. To this change was due in great measure the predominance of Arabic through out the Empire. Lastly, a regular post service was instituted from Damascus to the Provincial Capitals, especially destined for Government despatches. The Postmasters were charged with the task of informing the Caliph of all important news in their respective countries. Encyclop. Brit, vol. V p. 33. Périer's Hjjaj, p. 260 note (3). Jarrett's Suyuti, p. 226 note. Tr.]

since numerous Iraqians sought and found a safe asylum in Arabia for the evasion of punishment.

As soon as the successor of Omar arrived in Medina he demanded, on pain of death, the surrender of all the Iraqians there, declaring those as out-lawed who henceforward dared to receive or shelter an Iraqian refugee. The new governor of Mekka issued similar orders * Arabia also. Now shared the fate of the rest of the provinces where secret and public police, on the smallest suspicion, dealt at will with the life and property of the subject population. This position of affairs, resulting naturally in a sense of general insecurity, may have induced many to seek a military career—a career which now promised neither fame nor booty neither martyrdom nor paradise. To this fact, as also to the fact that there were many bands of men, belonging to the earlier rebel chiefs—bands now disbanded—we must, to a certain extent, ascribe the brilliant victories which were won almost simultaneously by Kutaiba on the other side of the Oxus; by Maslama, the brother of the Caliph in Armenia and Asia Minor; by Mohamed Ibn Kasim in India, and by Tarik and Musa in Spain and in Africa.

Kutaiba, the governor of Khorasan, reduced Sagan and several towns in Tokharistan to subjection; conquered the whole of the province of Bokhara with its capital; occupied Khawarizm (mod. Khiva) and Samarqand and the most important places in Farghana. His advanced posts were in Kashgar when he heard of the death of the Caliph. Belonging as he did to the party of Hajjaj he was afraid of being deposed by the successor of Walid, the Caliph Sulaiman, whom Hajjaj wanted to supplant in favour of a son of Walid. He therefore returned to Khorasan and there awaited orders from the New Caliph.

---

* [Hajjaj persuaded the Caliph to dismiss Omar in 712 and to appoint Othman B. Hayyan at Medina and Khalid at Kisri and Mekka. Tr.]

Mohamed Ibn Kasim reduced at first Mekran to subjection. He then proceeded south-east to Daibol, took it by storm and for three days abandoned it to the wrath and fury of his soldiery. This produced so great a terror among the inhabitants of Sind that they offered no further resistance but willingly submitted to his authority. He thus, without opposition, proceeded as far as the Indus. Here he defeated the prince Daher, conquered Daur and Bahmanabad, and then crossing the Hyphasis compelled the rich and well-fortified town of Multan to surrender after a long and obstinate siege. Just as Kashgar was the limit for the campaigns against China conducted by Kutaba; so was Multan the limit for Mohamed's conquests in India—limits set by the death of the Caliph. He, also, belonged to the party of Hajjaj who was, maltreated in the reign of Sulaiman, and ended his days, like a common criminal, in chains and in fearful torture.

Maslama, in certain measure, owed his success in Asia Minor and Armenia to the internal confusion of the Byzantine Empire under Justinian II, Phillipicus and Artemius. He and Abbas, a son of the Caliph, conquered Tayana, Heraklea, Samosata, Antioch in Pisidia, and penetrated north east as far as Erzrum and Derbend.

But by far the greatest success attended the military achievements of Musa and Tarik in Africa and Spain.*

Already under Abdul Malik, Musa had waged a murderous war against the Berbers, and by his victory on the banks of Malwiya, west of Tlemsen, had cleared the way for the conquest of Western Mauritania. Under Walid a great battle took place at Sus, ending in the victory of the Muslims, which was followed shortly by the occupation of Tangier. Tarik remained behind as governor of Tangier while Musa returned to Kairowan. Later on Tarik reduced to submission the whole of the country between

---

*[See, on the sons of Witiza, 'Arabic Spain' of Whishaw pp. 36 et seq. Tr.

Tangier and Tlemsen, and found in Count Julian who held Ceuta for the King of Spain an opponent not so easy to conquer as the wild Berber hordes. But here, as earlier in Egypt and Syria, the Arabs were favoured by internal dissensions among the Christians.

Apart from the fact that Count Julian belonged to the party of Witiza,* who shortly before had been hurled down from the throne by Roderik; bore had also a personal grudge against Roderik.

---

*[The facts regarding the Saracen invasion are shrouded in great obscurity. The contemporary records are extremely scanty, and it may be well to have in mind exactly what they amount to. The two primary sources are the chronicles that bear the names of Johannes Biclarensis and Isidorus Pacensis. John of Biclaro was of Gothic descent, and a native of the town of Scalabis, in Lusitania. He lived in the time of Leovigild, was celebrated for his great learning, and received his surname from the monastery of Biclaro, which he founded in Catalonia. His chronicle begins with the death of Athanagild in 567, and closes in 589, but from that point onward it has been continued by an unknown author down to the year 721. Regarding the period of the invasion its details are not only most meagre, but are liable to considerable doubt as to their authenticity; indeed they are believed to be largely due to the adoption of late marginal notes into the text. On the other hand, the work usually referred to as that of Isidore of Beja is very important. It is entitled "Epitoma Imperatorum, vel Arabum Ephemerides, atque Hispaniae Chronographia", and extends from the year 610 to the year 754 giving information not only regarding the Visigothic Kingdom, but also regarding Islam from the beginning of the Byzantine Empire from the time of Heraclires). For the time previous to the eighth century its sources are uncertain and its treatment of the early Visigothic kings is both scanty and unreliable. For the opening years of the eighth century it evidently leans on the continuation of John of Biclaro; but after that it becomes of the highest value, speaks freely, and may undoubtedly be accepted as the testimony of an eye witness......................Two other works, which the chronicler himself claims to have written, and which, had they been preserved, would have been of inestimable value, are now lost—Epitoma Temporum, dealing with the internecine strife of the Moslems in Spain; and 'Liber Verborem dierum saeculi', on the wars of Yusuf and his predecessors. The chronicle which we possess is in reality anonymous. It is

Thus the desire to avenge, combined with the hope that, with the help of the Arabs (from whom he never expected permanent settlement in Europe) he might again restore the throne to the sons of Witiza, led him on to negotiations with Tarik, and ultimately to an invitation to him to cross over to Spain.

As soon as Tarik was convinced that with the help of Julian and the numerous Spanish refugees, who were in communication with the enemies of Roderik, he would be able to conquer or at least to exploit this rich and fertile country—he made, in consultation with the Count, the necessary arrangements for crossing over. At first Tarif was ferried over with 500 men. He landed at a place subsequently named after him as Tarifa but, when he found no opposition, Tarik himself followed him with some 12000 men (May, 711) and took up a strong position on an elevation, called after him, Jabel Tarik, later on, disfigured into Gibralter. Theodmir, Commander of Andalusia, tried to oppose the Arabs, who now began to

---

practically a continuation of the history of the famous Isidore of Seville (560-636), and Dozy has conjectured, more or less plausibly, that the name now attached to it may have arisen through the error of some scribe, who, in copying the words 'Isidorus Hispalensis,' elided the first three letters of the adjective and wrote 'pacensis' for 'palensis.' The name Isidorus pacensis or Isidore of Beja ('Pax Julia') rests, according to Florez, on the authority of Juan Vaseo in the middle of the seventeenth century, who says he had found it in a manuscript which he had examined; but there is no internal ground for connecting the author with Beja. The writer, however, speaks so intimately and so exactly of Cordova that he probably, though not necessarily, may, as Dozy supposes, have lived there. Modern Spanish writers infer that he was a Christian who lived under the Arabs, first in Toledo, then in Cordova, and Senor Saavedra is content to call him simply 'El Anonimo Latino'. These two chronicles then, are all that may be properly denominated primary sources for the period. The next Christian record comes about seventy years after Isidore, and the nearest Arabic writer is removed from him about 120 years. His successors may frequently preserve early and correct traditions, but they cannot stand in the same rank of authority or be lightly accepted when they contradict him.

plunder the entire coast-land, but was defeated and compelled to summon Roderik to his aid. At this time Roderik was fighting the rebels in the North. He started as speedily as possible for the threatened South and collected a strong army in the neighbourhood of Cordova, to advance against Tarik, who in the meantime had also gathered together his scattered troops and strengthened himself by fresh reinforcements from Africa. The two armies met in the neighbourhood of the place called later, Xeres, and although the Christian army was numerically superior—almost twice the number—Tarik won the day. The muslims fought with religious enthusiasm and with the fury of despair. "Whither wouldst thou flee," Tarik called out to them: "the sea rages behind you, the enemy stand in front you." They fought like one man and they fought in perfect obedience to God and their commander; for thy felt that perseverence and victory would bring to them reward from above, military renown and rich booty; while cowardice

---

On the writer after Isidore cf Dahn, vi 686 seq, and Saavedra's interesting chapter, 'Las fuentes historicas.' It may be convenient to mention the more mportant Latin and Arabic writers in order.

Latin writers.	Arabic writers.
1. 'Chronicon Moissacense,' after 818 to 840.	1. Ibn Abdul Hakem, d. 871.
2. 'Chronicon Ovetense,' C 850.	2. Ahmad Rasi, d. 888 (7)
3. 'Chronicon Albedense', after 883.	3. Ahmad, Arrazi d. 936.
4. 'Gesta Samsonis abbatis Cordubae,' a little later.	4. His son Isa, called El Moro Rasis, ending 976.
5. Chronicle of Alfonso iii (d. 912) the so-called Sebastian of Salamanca, ending 866.	5. Ibn Alcotia (descendant of Witiza) d. 977.
6. The monk of Silo, 1110.	6. Akhbar Majmua, collections of traditions, c. 1006.
7. Archbishop Roderick Ximenes of Toledo, d. 1247.	7. Ibn Adhari, 'Al Bayan-ul-maghrib,' 1200.
8. Deacon Lucas of Tuy, in Galicia, d. 1250.	8. Nowairi, d. 1332.
	9. Al Makkari d. 1631. Tr.]

135

and defeat would mean divine wrath, disgrace, capture and death. Of very different stuff was the Christian army made up. It was composed partly of prisoners and serfs who had followed their masters under sheer compulsion. Victory could bring them no material prosperity, and defeat very little disgrace. Moreover even among the Spanish generals there were many friends of the fallen dynasty who like Count Julian wished defeat to the usurper, because in that event they hoped all the more quickly to raise the sons of Witiza to the throne. Thus, after several days of battle the Christian army was so thinned by the sword of the Arabs as also by famine and treason that when Roderick himself was missed (probably he perished in the waters of Guadelete) the whole army melted away like snow in sunshine and sought safety behind the walls.

Tarik, too, suffered considerable loss of troops. His army is said to have dwindled down to 9,000, but the news of his glorious victory and the immense booty thereby acquired speedily attracted to his banner other war-like people from Africa who more than made up the loss. Tarik, therefore, before the enemy had had time to recover from the shock of defeat, could pursue his victory. He himself reduced to submission Sidonia, Carmona, Eciya, and advanced towards Cordova; while other generals conquered Malaga, Granada and Orikuela. The conquered towns were to a large extent placed in charge of the Jews, on whose loyalty the Arabs could implicitly rely, for the fanaticism and greed of the Christian clergy had driven them to despair.* To these Jews, then, the Arabs,

---

*[See Whishaw's Arabic Spain pp. 38 and 39 notes. The dealings of the Gothic rulers and Churchmen with the Jews probably had no little influence in facilitating the success of the Moslems. For nearly a century before the conquest they had been subjected to a savage persecution. And almost every Council of Toledo, from the fourth (A. D. 633) onwards, legislated against them, until the seventeenth (694) enacted that they should all be made slaves and their goods confiscated. The whole of Book XII. Tit II of the *Fuero Juzgo* is filled

(who had granted them complete religious freedom and who were satisfied with a small capitation tax), were nothing more nor less than their protectors and saviours.

As the garrison of Cordova offered a stout and obstinate resistance and as a formal siege had to be laid—Tarik, made over the command of the besieging army to Mughith Al-Rumi and himself advanced towards Toledo. He clearly saw that the success of his military operations depended upon the conquest of the capital of the Visigothic empire before the Christians had had time to recover from terror and to unite again under a newly-elected sovereign. Mughith, however, soon took possession of Cordova; for he was shown by a prisoner a spot in the walls whence he could effect entrance into the town. After a siege of three months the garrison surrendered.

Tarik, in the meantime, proceeded to Toledo and to his great joy and not a little surprise, found very slight opposition there. The rich and influential inhabitants, here as in Cordova, had

---

with legislation of a persecuting nature. The Jews were forbidden to keep the Passover or their accustomed feasts and Sabbaths, to marry by Jewish rites, to eat their own food, to circumcise, and, whether baptised or not, to give evidence against Christians. The result was that when the invaders came, the Jews welcomed them, if they did not actually invite them over, as they were accused of doing in the reign of Egica. According to Makkari Cordova, Granada and the district of Rayah, to which Malaga belonged, were left in charge of the Jews after being taken, "and this practice became almost general in the succeeding years; for whenever the Moslems conquered a town, it was left in custody of the Jews, with only a few Moslems, the rest of the army proceeding to new conquests." Gayangos says, on the authority of Ibn Khaldun, that most of the Berber tribes inhabiting the northern shores of Africa professed the Jewish religion, and that, although the twelve thousand under Tarik's orders were said to have been previously converted to Islam, this conversion was not likely to have been so sincere as to blot out immediately all sympathy with their former co-religionists (Makkari, I. 280-531). Lucas of Tuy says that the Jews opened the gates of Toledo to the Moslems while the Christians were attending a service on Palm Sunday at the Church of St. Leocadia *extra urbem* (in Schott, IV. 70). Tr.]

18

left the town before his arrival, taking away their effects with them to Galicia. The scanty garrison, which had remained behind, perceived the absurdity and the futility of holding out against Tarik for any length of time, and therefore avoided by timely capitulation the terrible fate of the towns taken by force of arms. The main conditions of voluntary surrender here, as elsewhere, were: security of life and property (with the exception of horses and weapons) for those that remained behind in the town; freedom to leave, to those who desired to emigrate; absolute freedom to conduct divine service within the church; liberty to have recourse to their own ecclesiastical courts in matters of dispute among Christians. The Christians of course had to pay the capitation tax; to which was further added an annual tribute according to their possessions or the produce of their land. Tarik, who was anxious not only to conquer towns but also to amass riches, did not stay long in Toledo. A small garrison, with the help of the Jewish population sufficed, to guard the deserted town. Tarik with the *E'lite* of his troops, was thus able to pursue the flying Christians in the direction of Guadalaxara and to take possession of the valuables which with difficulty they carried along with them; among the finds, a golden table, set with pearls and precious stones, fills the first position. Then he continued his conquering campaign across the Castilian mountain chain as far as Astorga. Though subordinate to Musa, governor of Africa, Tarik had undertaken all these expeditions wholly on his own responsibility. According to some reports he had even carried on the later wars, contrary to the express orders of Musa, who, on hearing of the occupation of Cordova, is said to have ordered him to proceed no further until his arrival. Although the disobedience of Tarik had been crowned with brilliant results; still the envious Musa could not forgive him for forestalling him in the conquest of the Capital and in the seizure of immense treasures. Leaving, therefore, his son behind as his representative in Africa, he crossed over with a considerable number of troops to Spain. Not to be eclipsed by Tarik as a conqueror, he proceeded to Quadaliquer and conquered Sidonia, Seville and Merida. He took the first by storm; the second, through the treason of the Bishop Oppas; and the third, after violent resistance, by capitulation. At Toledo he met Tarik whom, at the very first meeting, he put in chains, like an ordinary criminal; though Tarik had tried to appease him by the gift of precious war-booty. After sometime, however, when the Caliph was informed of these happenings, Tarik was treated with well-deserved consideration. We find him again at the head of a division of troops proceeding, in a north-easterly direction, to Saragossa, while Musa himself advanced towards Salamanca. Then, changing his course, Musa also took the rôute to Saragossa where, effecting a junction with Tarik, he compelled the town to surrender. Thereupon the two generals parted again. Tarik followed the course along the Ebro, took Tortosa and then bent his steps southward, conquering Valencia, Xativa and Denia; while Musa attacked Catalonia. He is said even to have thought of crossing over the Pyrennees, when a messenger from the Caliph came to summon him to Damascus. Before his return he even undertook an expedition to Galicia and penetrated, devastating and burning towns, as far as Lugo; when came a second messenger from Damascus commanding him, in the name of the Caliph, instantly to leave Spain. Musa had acted as independently towards the Caliph as Tarik had done towards Musa. Without obtaining the sanction of the Caliph he had left his governorship to cross over to Andalusia. He was almost the lord of Spain and Africa and could, if he had so wished, easily have declared himself independent of the court of Damascus. At the court, where Tarik counted numerous friends; there was a strong prejudice against Musa, owing to his scandalous behaviour towards Tarik. According to some reports he set him at liberty only at the express command of the Caliph. Finally, Walid was anxious to enrich his treasury by the rich booty made in Spain, and on that account too Musa was asked to return and to render account to the Caliph. Before his return Musa divided the governorship of Spain and Africa among his sons. He appointed Abdul Aziz governor of Spain and fixed Seville as his residence—by reason of the close connection of this town with the Muslims of Africa. The governorship of Africa he made over to his sons Abdul Malik and Abdullah; the former was to administer the Western and the latter the Eastern portion of the African dominion. Then he crossed over to Ceuta, whence he took the land rôute, followed by countless slaves and prisoners. Besides these, 30 wagon-loads of valuables captured in Spain, and thousands of camels, constituted his slowly dragging train. Thus it took him more than a year to reach Fustat (December 714) where, at the instance of the Caliph, he was received by the Prefect and other influential residents of the town. Thus, day by day, in leisurely marches, did he continue his triumphal procession, until he reached Tiberias. Here he learnt that the Caliph lay seriously ill. Anxious perhaps to close his reign with a splendid triumph; possibly also to secure a portion of the valuable booty for his family, he summoned Musa in writing to hasten his journey. At the same time Musa was asked by Sulaiman to delay his entry into Damascus as long as possible; for he too was eager to adorn and glorify his accession with the very same trophies of war.

Musa, possibly disbelieving the seriousness of Walid's illness, or perhaps expecting a better reception at his hands than at those of Sulaiman, would not listen to Sulaiman's suggestion. On arrival in Damascus, however, he found the Caliph in his last stage (February 715)—thus, without any protection, he found himself exposed to the wrath of the new Sovereign. He was accused of dividing the booty, contrary to the provisions of the Qur'an, and of claiming as his own many of the military achievements which were really Tarik's and not his at all—among others the one that resulted in the capture of the far-famed table referred to above. He was, according to some reports, heavily fined and sent to prison—nay, even for sometime publicly exposed to the burning sun. Even, at the instance of Sulaiman, the head of his son Abdul Aziz, slain in Spain, was shown to him, and he was asked if he knew whose it was? Musa who was then in his 78th year and had nothing more to fear, is said to have thus replied: Indeed I do know whose head it is. It is the head of the man who performed his prayer at early dawn and who fasted a great deal. May the curse of God be on him— if he was not a better man than his murderer. According to contemporary reports which recount many an act of hideous barbarity; Musa is said to have died a pauper among his kinsmen. On the contrary, according to other reports he was forgiven by the Caliph, and died on his way to Mekka on pilgrimage.

Of his comrade in arms, Tarik, who left Spain almost at the same time, we know that Sulaiman at one time thought of appointing him Governor of Spain, but again abandoned his resolution fearing that, highly popular as he was with the troops, he might found an independent dynasty there. The Islamic empire had now attained so stupendous a size that the Caliphs considered it dangerous to entrust distant provinces to men who might enthral and capture the affection of the troops placed under their charge. Over the subsequent career of Tarik there hangs a veil of obscurity. It is probable that he ended his days in peaceful seclusion—away from the clash of arms and the din of party faction.

III. *Disunion within the Empire and beginning of the decline and fall—from Sulaiman to Hisham.*

Fear of a possible revolt of the governors and the necessity, arising therefrom, of appointing near relatives of the Caliphs or mere phantoms as governors, weakened the empire no less than inner discord and feuds; notably, the deep-seated division and disunion between the Yamanides *i.e.* the South Arabian and the Mudarites *i.e.*, the North Arabian tribes. The Caliphs now favoured the one and now the other party. The Mudarites, to whom Hajjaj and his subordinate governors, belonged, had their day under Walid. But, as already mentioned, Sulaiman, having been supplanted by the Mudarites, joined the Yamanides; when he rose to power. Yazid Ibn Muhallab was then their chief, and, as such, treated Mohamed, the conqueror of India, as a common criminal, and paved the way for a similar fate for Qutaiba, the conqueror of Transoxiana. Towards Qutaiba, the governor of Khorasan, he had to proceed, however, with greater care and circumspection than against Mohamed and Musa. Musa was away from his army. Mohamed, taken unawares in Sind by his successor Muawiya Ibn Muhallab, had neither the means nor the opportunity for revolt. He was forthwith sent in chains to Wasit where, along with the other relatives of Hajjaj, he suffered an agonising death. But Qutaiba was, in the midst of his loyal troops and in a province which was ever and anon ready to raise the standard of revolt. Further he was as experienced as a statesman as he was powerful as general. Upon the advice of Yazid, Sulaiman sent him a massage in writing in which, without expressly confirming him in his post, he, commanded him to arrange for yet another expedition to Ferghana, with a view to its complete conquest. But the

142

messenger was also the bearer of a second letter to the army in which a higher salary was promised to them and liberty was given to every soldier either to join the campaign or to return home. This was intended, on the one hand, to humour the army, and on the other, to withdraw from Qutaiba those who were weary of a long war in a distant land or those who were anxious to return home.

Qutaiba saw through the intention of the Caliph when he was informed of the contents of the second letter. He declared the messenger to be a traitor who was striving to weaken the army by means of a forged and fictitious letter. Thereupon he wrote three letters to the Caliph and he sent them all through one and the same messenger. In the first he described his loyalty and devotion to the House of Omayya and begged the Caliph to confirm him in his post; assuring him that he would serve Sulaiman as loyally and zealously as he had served his two predecessors. In the second letter he reminded the Caliph of his brilliant military triumphs, spoke slightingly of the family of Muhallab and declared that if Yazid was appointed governor of Khorasan he would resist him by force of arms. In the third he simply renounced allegiance to the Caliph. The messenger was advised to deliver only the first letter to the Caliph. The second he was to deliver in case the Caliph communicated the contents of the first to Yazid, and the third, after the second had been made over to Yazid.

The Caliph, whom the messenger found sitting by the side of Yazid, showed the first two letters to his favourite. The third, according to some reports, he is said to have kept to himself; according to others he is said to have flung it to Yazid with those words: "We have unjustly insulted Qutaiba, he is a useful man." On the following day, the Caliph sent back the messenger to Merv along with another, who was entrusted with

143

**

the letter of confirmation to Qutaiba as governor of Khorasan. Qutaiba, possibly, fearing that too much delay might cause disaffection among his troops, took up arms against the Caliph, without awaiting the return of his messenger. Hearing at Hulwan that Qutaiba had renounced allegiance to the Caliph, the royal messenger forthwith returned to Damascus. Qutaiba (on obtaining from his messenger the account of what had happened at Damascus) repented of having unnecessarily rebelled against the Caliph. He, however, placed too great a reliance upon his troops, to either submit or to beg for mercy from the Caliph, or, as one of his brothers counselled him, to go over, with the pick of his troops, to Transoxiana. The time for mutiny and insurrection, however, had gone by. There were only too many instances and they were well within the recollection of the soldiers—instances of unsuccessful rebellion. Moreover they clearly saw that even in the event of success the advantages would not be for them but for their Chiefs. When Qutaiba, therefore, summoned the troops to renounce the Caliph; his summons met with sullen silence. This annoyed him to such an extent that he forthwith burst into a volley of abuse; particularly directed against the ungrateful Beduins, to whom he said that, as beggars he had received them into the army, and had enriched them with the plunder of the valuable properties of the Turkish and Persian Princes. These words enraged and alienated the Beduins, who now joined the Yamanides that were in the army. It was not long before some leaders, loyal to the Caliph and hankering after high posts, put themselves at their head. Qutaiba, (instead of arresting the leaders of the conspiracy, permitted the disloyal ones of the troops to withdraw) made a second speech to the assembled army, a speech as fruitless and barren of result as the first one; and only when it was too late did he show an inclination to proceed against them with strong and vigorous measures. He was attacked in his palace and was killed by a Yamanide who sent his head to Damascus (715).

Yazid, the successor of Qutaiba, hitherto the governor of Iraq, persecuted the followers of his predecessor in office and made himself, by cruelty and oppression, as he had already done in Iraq, no less odious and hateful than Hajjaj. But devoted, as he was, to pleasure and enjoyment, he yet aspired to win distinction by military glory. He therefore undertook an expedition to the Provinces of Jurjan and Tabaristan where, even prior to him, excursions had been made but no lasting conquests effected. Tabaristan was made to pay tribute and Jurjan, after it had broken the peace, was conquered with force, and the capital, bearing the same name as the province, was, after a siege of seven months, taken by storm. This feat of arms is almost the only military glory which adorned the reign of Sulaiman. The Muslims, in other spheres, were either inactive or unsuccessful. In India they could not maintain the earlier conquests except Sind, which they held with a great deal of trouble and exertion. In Spain, not only all further conquest was checked, in consequence of the murder of Abdul Aziz, at once a warrior and a statesman and the subsequent deposition of his cousin Ayyub; but this change of governorship, giving birth, as it did, to disputes and division, emboldened the Christians of the highlands of Asturia, Galicia and Navarre in their opposition; an opposition which shortly after, under the leadership of Pelagius, became very terrible to the Muslims. In the war against the Byzantines, however, the Arabs suffered the severest defeat. The mutiny of the fleet against their Admiral John, the dethronement of the Emperor Anastasius and the war of Leo, the Isaurian, against him—all these, were of good augury to the Arabs, who after occupying several of the fortified places in Asia minor, laid siege to Constantinople both by sea and by land under the leadership of Maslama, a brother of the Caliph. But Leo, who was hitherto solicitous of the friendship of the Arabs and had promised them a portion of the Empire, on ascending the throne, treated them as an enemy to be conquered

145

19

and crushed and utterly annihilated. Greek fire and a violent
storm destroyed a portion of the fleet at anchor, as also a portion
of the fleet which had set sail from Syria, laden with provisions for
the besieging army. There soon arose a terrible famine, followed
by a devastating pestilence. The condition of the Arabs became
so pitiable that even the Greeks in Asia Minor took courage and
attacked the thin Muslim ranks * Thus after the death
of Sulaiman (Sept.—Oct. 717) they received orders to return
home—by far the greater portion of the army having perished †.
Undecided and on the point of death, Sulaiman, at the instance
of Raya B. Haywa, a reputed scholar,‡ appointed his pious cousin,
for many years Governor of Egypt, Omar Ibn Abdul Aziz, his
successor to the Caliphate, and indeed, on this occasion, a
further innovation was introduced; namely the rendering of
homage to the successor in the life time of the Caliph but
without the disclosure of his name.§ To the very end Sulamian

* [See, Bury's Later Roman Empire Vol. II 401 Sqq; Finlay's History of
Greece, Vol. II; Weil's Geschichte der Chalifen I, 565 Sqq; Gibbon, Bury's
Ed. Vols. V and VI Tr.]

† [Of an army of 180,000 only, 30,000 (land army) returned, according to
Arab sources. Paul the Deacon, the Lombard historian, makes the number of
those who died 300,000! By the time numbers reached Italy, they were beyond
recognition. Tr.]

‡ [See Ibn Athir, Vol. 5, 27; Masudi, V, 417; Hammer-Purgstall, Litt.
Gesch. der Araber, II 131; Weil, Gesch. der Chalifen 1,574-577. He died in
A.H. 112 (A.D. 730) Tr.].

§ [Fakhri tells us that when Sulaiman was attacked with the illness of
which he died he resolved to proclaim one of his sons as Caliph. A Councillor
of his (Raya) dissuaded him from this course, and said to him "O, Amir, one of
the safeguards against the torments of the grave for the Caliph is the nomi-
nation by him of a successor who is pious and who can take care of his
subjects."............Then he consulted his adviser as to the succession of Omar
Ibn Abdul Aziz. This met with his approval. Sulaiman, therefore, wrote out
and sealed his last will and testament. He then sent for the members of his
family and told them " swear allegiance to him whom I have appointed in my
will" but he did not mention the name. When Sulaiman died Raya, concealing

intended to leave the throne to one of his sons; thus the credit, so highly esteemed by the Arabs, of having brought a man such rs Omar II. to the throne, belongs more to Raya than to the Caliph Sulaiman himself.

Indeed, even, the Muslim biographers find very little to praise in Sulaiman. The joys of the harem and the table—which were responsible for his early death—interested him more than the welfare of his subjects. As under his predecessor architecture, and under his successor the Qur'an and the traditions constituted the subject-matter of popular talk—so under him the most favourite topics of conversation were dainty dishes and sporting women.* Moreover he was greedy, cruel, jealous to a degree.

In everything Omar II. was different from his predecessor, and it is beyond doubt that he owed the Caliphate less to Sulaiman than to the man who attended him in his last days—even if there was no actual tampering with his will. The sons and brothers of the deceased were quite taken aback when the will was made known to them—still they gave in, for they had already sworn allegiance to the Caliph-elect. Even an absent son of Walid who asserted his claims to the Caliphate yielded the moment he learnt that Omar occupied the place of his father. Universal was the esteem in which he was held, by reason of the purity of his life, and signally so at the time when he was the governor of Medina.

The possession of power did not in any way corrupt him. and both as a prince and as a private gentleman he may worthily take his rank by the side of the great Caliph Omar I, but

---

the fact of Sulaiman's death, convened those very persons and told them "to swear allegiance a second time. They did so and when satisfied that the whole proceeding was in perfect order he made known to them the fact of Sulaiman's death. Al-Fakhri, p. 206. [French Tr.]

* [Al-Fakhri, (Arabic text) p. 151 ; De Goeje, Frag. Hist Arb. p. 11 Tr.]

unlike Omar I he did not thirst for the conquest of new countries. For him it was a matter of greater moment to attend to the preservation and prosperity of the conqured countries than to extend more and more the frontier of the Islamic Empire. Omar clearly saw that a further splitting up of power could not but be ruinous to the Empire, and he accordingly strove, by justice and clemency, to win the subject races over to Islam. All Governors accused of oppression and extortion were at once replaced by others. Yazid, the son of Muhallab, who had latterly forfeited the favour of Sulaiman, was forthwith recalled from Khorasan and sent to prison for squandering away public money. His successor Jarrah was likewise deposed for having exacted from the neo-converts capitation-tax on the pretext that their conversion was not genuine. Unlike his predecessors the pious Omar would not aggrandise or enrich the Muslim Empire at the cost of unbelievers. Conviction and not violence was the motto upon which he uniformly acted. To the people of other faiths—he was uniformly just and generous.

Under his Caliphate Islam made the greatest advance among the inhabitants of India and Africa, and even in Spain where he appointed the clement and statesmanlike Samah, in the place of the cruel Al-Hurr, whose inroads in Gallia were more of the character of predatory expeditions than permanent conquests, the number of conversions grew with a remarkable rapidity.

Omar was dominated by one thought, and that was to concentrate the Islamic Empire into one compact whole. He was prepared to throw up the distant provinces—making them as the places of residence of the unbelievers within the bosom of the Islamic Empire. Thus in pursuance of this policy the troops from Transoxiana were to be recalled and Sind was to form the Eastern frontier of the Empire; while Samah was to assign to the Christians of Spain specially the lands to the north of that

148

country. But Omar's Caliphate was far too brief to carry through a scheme of so great a magnitude. However, it did one thing—it tended to hold up his predecessors more and more to contempt and presumably also his successor Yazid II, appointed by Sulaiman, as second in order of succession. Yazid was in no way like Omar, and had already before his accession made himself hateful to many. The feeling against him ran so high that even in the reign of Omar II the Kharijites conspired together in Iraq and called upon him to alter the last will of Sulaiman. Omar is said to have requested of them three days' time to consider the matter, but before the expiration of the three days he died. His death, therefore, naturally raises the suspicion that he was poisoned at the instance of Yazid or some one of his party. (February 720).

Yazid II was as unlike Omar II as he was unlike Sulaiman. Despising the pleasures of this life and striving to do nothing save to serve God with all his heart, Omar II looked upon this life as a mere period of probation for the one beyond the grave. Yazid, on the other hand, gave himself up to the joys of life—to wine, women and song—heedless of his own soul and careless of the prosperity and welfare of the state. He was distinguished from Sulaiman specially in this that while Sulaiman favoured the Yamanides; cruelly persecuting the Mudarites, particularly the branch to which Hajjaj belonged and which sought to supplant him from the throne; Yazid on the other hand again set Mudarites—from which came his mother—at the head of the state, with the result that the Yamanides—notably the family of Muhallab—were now exposed to their wrath and fury.

Yazid, the son of Muhallab, clearly saw the position of affairs. While Omar lay dying he fled from the prison to which Omar had consigned him, and successfully made his escape to Basra. The Governor of the Caliph, refusing to allow him admission was beaten back by the supporters of Muhallab and was compelled to retire into the fort. But even this was taken by storm and the brother of Yazid, therein imprisic¬ed, was restored to liberty. At Basra, Yazid found support only in his tribesmen and the common-folk, who fondly joined every insurrection that took place.

Mindful of the terrible consequences—still fresh in their minds —the rest of the population were not prepared to sacrifice their lives and property for a man whom even the pious and forgiving Omar had deprived of his liberty. Many left the town, others remained behind without being seduced into treason by the hypocritical speeches of a man noted alike for his cruelty and debauchery.

Nevertheless homage was done to him at Basra, and his supporters were considerably re-inforced from Persia where the Omayyads were never really liked. Even Wasit now went over to him, and the governor could only keep Kufa in check with difficulty. Soon, however, under the leadership of the brave Maslama an army started from Syria. It completely routed the rebels at Aqr, in the neighbourhood of Kufa, on the left bank of the Euphrates. Yazid himself fell in battle, along with his two brothers. The rest of his relatives and kinsmen were either slain in their flight to India or were taken captives and sold as slaves.

It is probable that, to this rebellion, the suppression of which cost the best Syrian troops of the Caliph, we must ascribe the failure of the governors of Yazid against the enemies abroad. The governors were left entirely to their own resources in their warfare against them.

The army in Transoxiana suffered a frightful defeat, that in Armenia was attacked by the Khosars and even the second batch led against them by Jarrah was forced to retreat. Some victories were won in Asia Minor, but, at an enormous sacrifice.

Even in Africa the change of government had very pernicious results. The newly-apppointed governor adopted a policy of oppression and cruelty not only towards the descendants of Musa and Muhallab but also towards the Berbers. He was eventually murdered. His successor was a governor, chosen by the people, whom the Caliph, at first confirmed but subsequently replaced by another.

Spain, being independent of the governor of Africa, (where, about this time, the authority of the Caliph stood on an insecure footing) was not very much directly affected by the happenings in Africa; still the anarchical conditions could scarcely have failed to exercise an unfavourable effect there also. The necessary reinforcements from Africa and Arabia were not forthcoming, and the existing apparatus of war was hardly in keeping with the adventurous projects and undertakings of the commanders. Thus it was that the expedition of Samah to the other side of the Pyrenees (720-21) in the reign of Yazid, ended disastrously at the battle of Toulouse, and the Muslims were compelled to retire again to Narbonne. The defeat at Toulouse, the first which Christian Europe inflicted upon the Arabs, undoubtedly nerved the Christian population of Spain and the surviving members of the royal house to fresh resistance. About this time also took place the first wars of Pelagius against the Arabs, which led to the foundation of a new Christian Empire and eventually to the overthrow of the Arab power in Spain.*

---

* [In India several provinces, says Prof. De Goeje, which had been converted to Islam under Omar II, declared themselves independent because the promise of equal rights for all Muslims was not kept under the reign of his successors. This led to the evacuation of the Eastern part of India (called Hind by the Arabs, Sind being the name of the Western part) and to the founding of the strong cities of Mahfusa and Mansura for the purpose of controlling the land. Tr.]

**

The Caliphate of Yazid lasted only four years. To him succeeded (January, 724) his brother Hisham, already marked out for the throne by popular choice. He was not only free from the vices which disfigured the character of his predecessor, but he was also conspicuous for his clemency, piety and love of justice. He had to pay, however, for the faults of Yazid and during his reign of twenty years not only had he to fight with insurrections at home but also against external enemies and rebellious frontier-provinces.

The split, between the Yamanides and the Mudarites in the Caliphate of Sulaiman and Yazid, unceasingly fostered and nourished by the emissaries of the Hashimites (i. e. the members of the family of the Prophet who continually preached rebellion against the Omayyads) was a misfortune of portentous magnitude for the Empire. Moreover two characteristic vices of Hisham added fuel to the fire and betrayed him into numerous perplexities. Hisham was suspicious and close-fisted. In a corrupt age, such as his and among a people ruled by love of riches and revenge, these vices must have been pernicious, nay, perilous to a degree. If Hisham's greed held him back, from placating his friends by substantial gifts; his suspicious nature lent too ready an ear to the tittletattle of every revengeful liar. This led him only too frequently to acts of violence and constant changes in governorships.

The first Governor of Hisham in Iraq was Khalid Ibn Abdullah Al-Qisri. He was a Yamanide, and he therefore began his governorship with a most cruel persecution of his predecessor Omar Ibn Hubaira, the Mudarite, who was eventually killed by his order. By this he incurred the wrath and the hatred of the entire Mudarite tribe who, on that account, eagerly joined the agitators, working in the cause of the family of the Prophet. Thus there were frequent rebellions which could only be suppressed with the greatest possible difficulty.

The successor of Khalid, Yusuf Ibn Omar, was again a Mudarite. He, in turn, compelled Khalid, by means of rack and torture, to yield up to him his hoarded wealth. Not satisfied with what he got, and hoping to squeeze out more riches still, he sent him into prison, from which, after eighteen months, he was released by the Caliph.

The enquiry set up by Yusuf into the administration of Khalid had very fateful consequences for the Omayyad dynasty—consequences which were preparatory to their fall. When called upon to account for a sum of money which was missing from the treasury; Khalid, under torture, declared that he had placed it in the custody of Zaid Ibn Ali Ibn Husain, a great grandson of the son-in-law of the Prophet. Zaid denied this allegation, but, at the instance of the Caliph, had to go to Iraq to take his trial along with Khalid. This step caused a breach between Zaid and the Caliph, as also between Zaid and Yusuf, and was the occasion of his residence in Kufa. There he married a lady of Yamanide descent. This union brought him into closer connexion with the Yamanides who hated the new governor. Despite the warning of his friends, Zaid put himself forward as a claimant to the throne and secretly secured the homage of the Shiites. Yusuf, however, adopted effectual measures to stifle this mutiny in the bud, and Zaid atoned for his ambition with his blood. Later his son, Yahya, also perished in Khorasan together with many of the supporters of his family.

But the repeated failure of the Alides to succeed in their effort emboldened the Abbasids to seek their own fortune. Hitherto the claims of the Alides had stood in their way. They could not dare to work single-handed. They had to cast their lot with the Alides and had to work in concert with them—for the family of the Prophet—to which they, as the descendants of his uncle, belonged as much as did the Alides, the descendants of his daughter. The whole of Iraq was now prepared to support

153

the cause of the Abbasids. One of their active emissaries made in Kufa the acquaintance of Abu Muslim who, as we shall see later, paved the way for the success of the Abbasids.

In the Caliphate of Hisham far more tumultuous than in Iraq were affairs in Khorasan. Open warfare between the Mudarites and the Yamanides, mutiny of the natives who were encouraged and inflamed by the missionaries of the Abbasids, and unsuccessful expeditions to Transoxiana, followed one after another.

Things went so far that even Muslim generals formed alliances with the unfaithful to bring about the fall of the hateful governor, and not until the brave and circumspect Nasr Ibn Sayyar was appointed to the governorship of Khorasan (738) was peace again restored. Even in India the oppression of the governors called forth much discontent. Many of the conquests slipped out of Muslim hands, and the Muslims were compelled to found the strong cities of Mahfuza and Mansurah to secure a base of operation and a place of refuge.*

On the north and the north-western frontiers of the Empire the Arabs had the greatest difficulty in maintaining the earlier boundary, although there was no internal trouble there. The strength of the Caliphate was too deeply shattered ; the Beduins, becoming rich and luxurious in the earlier wars, longed for peace and pleasure, and were reluctant to suffer any longer the fatigue and privations of warfare. Religious zeal was already on the wane ; nor was the desire for glory and renown and national greatness, evoked and sustained by inner unity or unwavering devotion to the head of the state.

In Adharbaijan the Muslims suffered several defeats which, however, were avenged with a great deal of bloodshed by Maslamah, the brother of the Caliph, but it cost that heroic

---

* [See Houtsma's Ency of Islam.]

general his life (732). Merwan, the later Caliph, who became at this time the governor of Armenia and Adharbaijan, confined his energies to the reduction of the frontier provinces between Tebriz, Erzrum and Eriwan.

In Asia Minor the Muslims were more successful, since Leo, the Isaurian, was wholly occupied with the internal affairs of the Byzantine Empire. They conquered Caesarea in Cappadocia (725—6) and advanced as far as Nicaea which they failed to occupy. In the following years they repeated their incursions by sea and by land, but they were finally beaten back in 730 by the Emperor at Acronium.

Affairs in Africa and Spain pointed most conclusively to the inability and inefficiency of the government. The ties of obedience and allegiance weakened more and more. In Africa the Berbers rose against the government—the reason being that the governors and officials, in spite of their conversion, worried and oppressed them, as they did the non-muslims. They joined hands with the Kharijites, who found a favourable soil to work upon in the existing antipathy of the Berbers to the rule of the Arabs and in their anxiety for political independence. Many an Arab army was destroyed. The whole of western Africa passed into the possession of the rebels, and even Kairowan, the seat of government, was very nearly captured.

In Spain the Arabs were victorious in the first years of Hisham's Caliphate. Hisham appointed Anbasa governor. He crossed the Pyrenees to avenge the defeat suffered by Samah and took Caracassone and Rimes, his army devastating the whole of Southern France. But these conquests were soon lost when Anbasa was killed (726) and the frequent transfer of governors, who were now Yamanides and now Mudarites, not only made large undertakings an impossibility but even called forth repeated insurrections at home. Not until 731 when Abdul Rahman Ibn Abdullah became governor did things improve in Spain. It

155

was he who had saved the beaten army at Toulouse from total wreck. He was loved both as a general and as an administrator. To begin with, he chastised the former governor Othman Ibn Abi Nesa, called Munuza by the Christians, who had refused obedience to him and had concluded an alliance with Duke Eudó of Aquitaine. Having done this he crossed the Pyrenees, with an immense army. Without meeting any serious resistance he advanced as far as Bordeaux. He conquered this town, crossed the Dordogne, and won a victory over Count Eudo. He then devastated Libourne and Poitiers and advanced, plundering and destroying, as far as Tours.

Charles Martel, having been appealed to by Count Eudo, now took the field against Abdul Rahman. After several days fight the Franks won a victory over the Arabs. It was thus— a division of the Frankish troops advanced against the Moorish Camp; the Arabs, instead of maintaining their ground, left the scene of action and hastened away for fear of losing their captured treasures. Abdul Rahman was killed, and his beaten army fled during the night, anxious for nothing else but to lodge their rich booty safely behind the walls of Narbonne.

Abdul Malik Ibn Kattan, the successor of Abdul Rahman, was to restore the glory of the Muslim arms in Gaul. But before doing so he had to subdue the rebellious districts of Catalonia, Arragon and Navarre. He was however beaten by the Christian hill-tribes. Moreover, complaints were made against his numerous acts of oppression. He was accordingly deposed (734). Not until Uqba was Gaul again flooded by Arab hordes and then indeed it was by the help of the Dukes and Counts of Septimania. They occupied Arles, Avignon, Valence and Lyon, and overran a portion of Burgundy and Dauphine. But after having brought the war against the Saxons to a successful termination, Charles Martel advanced, a second time, against the Arabs. The Lombards under Childebrand and Luitprand took Avignon by storm and the Arabs were driven back afresh to Narbonne, from whence they soon retired to the Rhône. In 739 Charles Martel once more forced them to beat a retreat. This defeat was followed by a civil war even in Spain in consequence of a despute between Abdul Malik Ibn Kattan, the successor of Uqba, and one Balj who had came over from Africa and claimed the governorship.*

These dissensions continued, with little interruption, until a scion of the House of Omayya, after the overthrow of the Omayyad dynasty, became the ruler of Andalus.†

---

* [Houtsma, Ency. of Islam.]

† [The Arabs had conquered Spain in 711 ; in 720 they had crossed the Pyrenees and seized Septimania which was a dependency of the Kingdom of the Visigoths. Using this as a base they had invaded Gaul. Eudo, duke of Aquitaine, had succeeded by his able policy in holding them in check for some years, but in 732 a new *Wali* or Governor Abd-ar-Rahman, belonging to a sect of extreme fanatics, resumed the offensive. Eudo was vanquished on the banks of the Garonne, Bourdeaux was taken and its churches burnt, and the Arabs then advanced by way of the Gap of Poitiers, towards the north. Poitiers resisted their attack, but the basilica of St Hilary, situated outside the walls, was burnt. Without halting, 'Abd-ar-Rahman continued his march on Tours, the resting place of the body of St. Martin, which was as it were the religious capital of Gaul. Eudo besought the aid of Charles, who hurried up and posted himself at the junction of the Clain and the Vienne. The two armies halted, facing one another, for seven days. Then, on an October Saturday of 732—exactly a hundred years after the death of Mahomet—the battle was joined, and Charles came off victorious. Abd-ar-Rahman was slain on the field. This battle became extremely celebrated and it is chiefly on account of it that later Chronicles give to Charles the surname of Tudites or Martellus (Charles Martel).

The day of Poitiers marks the turning point in the fortunes of the Arabs. Harassed during their retirement by Eudo and his Aquitanians, they met with defeat after defeat. But to crown all, at this moment internal dissensions broke out within the Arab Empire. The Maddites, regained the ascendency at the expense of their enemies the Yemenites, but the Berbers in Africa refused to obey the new rulers and rose in revolt. The Arabs, occupied with

We shall revert to this subject later. For the present, it is enough to state that under Hisham the Muslims lost whatever they had conquered in Gaul, and that in the closing years of his reign perfect anarchy prevailed through out Syria.

Thus it was that, in spite of many good qualities which Hisham undoubtedly possessed, the Omayyad dynasty lost more and more in position and in prestige. Nor was its future reassuring; for Walid II, his successor-elect (the son of Yazid II) was hated and despised for his low passions and hideous vices, which boldly set at defiance all laws and morality.

Hisham tried to appoint his son Maslamah in place of Walid as his successor, but there was not much to choose between them. He was not very much better than Walid, and both Khalid, the governor of Iraq, and Merwan dissuaded Hisham from carrying his intention into effect. They pointed out to him that by altering the arrangement effected by Yazid he would at once unleash dangerous passions and provoke serious dissensions. Hisham, therefore, abandoned his intentions and hoped to mend the ways of his successor by adopting a rigorously severe policy towards him. But all his resolutions remained fruitless and ineffective. Walid had friends at Court who secretly supported

---

the suppression of this rebellion, were thenceforth unable to throw powerful armies into Gaul.

Charles proceeded to take the offensive against the Muslims. In 737 he wrested from them the town of Avignon which they had seized, and then attempted the conquest of Septimania but in spite of strenuous efforts he was unable to effect the capture of Narbonne. He had to content himself with laying waste the country systematically and destroying the fortifications of Agde, Beziers and Maguelonne. He set fire to the amphitheatre at Nîmes, and marks of the fire are still visible. In 739, the Arabs having attempted a new descent on Provence and even threatened Italy, Charles marched against them once more and drove them out. He allied himself against them with Luitprand, King of the Lombards, who adopted the Frankish ruler according to the Germanic custom. Cambridge Medieval History Vol. II. pp. 128-129. Tr.]

and encouraged him. One of these caused everything to be locked up and sealed in the name of Walid as soon as Hisham died (6th Feb. 743)—Walid being at the time in the country, touring about with his carousing companions. Thus, to warm water for washing the dead body of the Caliph they had to borrow a kettle.

IV. Further decline and fall of the Omayyads—from Walid II to Merwan II.

Though it was a matter of common knowledge that Walid II had hitherto indulged in every form of sensual pleasure ; that he had violated, with impunity, every single precept of the Qur'an ; and had even gone on pilgrimage to Mekka accompanied by dogs and well-stocked with wine ;—yet, in spite of all, he was saluted as Caliph. People hastened to him at Damascus to offer their allegiance to him, because every one was eager to have his share of the treasure amassed and left by Hisham. The Caliph did not disappoint the expectations which the people had formed of his generosity. Indeed he hoped to secure the loyalty of the troops by increasing their pay ; believing, that with their aid, he could eventually crush not only the populace but the members of his own family too. This very unbeliever, who freely gave himself up not only to hunting, wine and music, but to all manner of unspeakable vices, issued a rescript in which, in the name of God and his Prophet, he called for unconditional obedience, laying down obedience to the Caliph as one of the fundamental principles of Islam ; and furthermore, summoned the people to do homage to his two sons as future Caliphs.

This rescript, fringed and adorned with pious sayings and passages from the Qur'an, uttering at once threats of hell-fire and holding out promise of Paradise, stirred up the greatest resentment. The popular wrath waxed fiercer and fiercer, because of the minority of the sons of the Caliph, and even men who would have nothing whatever to do with a rebellion, could not very well make up their minds to do homage to two boys who were neither fit to pray nor to act as competent witnesses to any transaction, religious or secular. But the most aggrieved of all were the Omayyad princes who had hoped later to ascend the throne; for, since the Caliph Abdul Malik, none had appointed his own sons as successors.

To the many disasters to which the royal house was exposed since the Caliphate of Sulaiman there was now added one of deep and far-reaching consequence—the want of unity within the domestic circle. The sons of Hisham and Walid I—smarting under personal wrongs—joined the enemies of the Omayyads, who regarded the reigning Caliph in the light of an unbeliever, a free-thinker, guilty of incestuous intercourse and, as such, unworthy of the obedience of the faithful. But the worst thing for Walid was that on his mother's side, he was a near kinsman of the evil-famed Hajjaj, and as such he took up definitely the side of the Mudarites, exposing the Yamanides to their wrath and fury. Thus Khalid, the former Governor of Khorasan, who had been set at liberty in the last years of the Caliphate of Hisham, and was living peacefully at Damascus, was handed over for a sum of 50,000,000 Dirhams to his enemy Yusuf Ibn Omar, who had long been thirsting for his blood. Yusuf carried his cruelty to such an extent that he had Khalid, in a woollen shirt, on an unsaddled camel, brought up to Kufa where, partly out of vengeance, partly in the hope of extorting from him a confession regarding concealed treasures, he had him torn from limb to limb, until death released him from his agony.

For the Yamanides, however, more painful even than the terrible murder of Khalid was a satire, in which the Yamanide tribes, the Kinsmen of Khalid, were held up to scorn and obloquy for their weakness and cowardice, and were branded as vulgar and wretched slaves, who after abandoning Khalid to his fate, meekly submitted to every form of humiliation and indignity. To heighten the effect of this satire, by which an enemy of the Caliph obviously strove to urge the Yamanides on to vengeance, Walid himself was set down as its author.

When Yazid, a son of Walid I, was satisfied that he would obtain the support of the Yamanides in a war against the Caliph, he resolved to dethrone him. In vain did his brother Abbas, the Governor of Armenia, (later Caliph Merwan II) orally and in writing, try to dissuade him from a course which was sure to precipitate the fall of the entire dynasty. In vain did they implore him not to set up, with his own hands, by renouncing allegiance, a conflagration which must destroy them all, and which must necessarily forward the cause of the enemies of their family. The power-seeking Yazid closed his ears to all the admonitions administered to him and went on, in spite of his brother, who had threatened to bring his conduct to the notice of the Caliph, to preach insurrection against the Caliph in the name of God and the imperilled faith.

When he had secured a large number of the population of the Capital and the surrounding districts, he took possession at night of a mosque in which a good stock of arms and weapons were stored. These he divided among his followers. Thereupon he caused the arrest of the Governor of Damascus and the chief of the body-guard, with the result that even those who were friendly to the Caliph (who at that time was in the neighbourhood of the Dead Sea) found themselves without a leader. By bribery he also managed to seduce some 5 to 6000 troops whom he led against the Caliph. Informed of these happenings, the Caliph, after a long consultation with his companions, decided to retire to the strong castle of Najra and there await Yazid, hoping that his troops would soon gather round him. But a portion of his troops who, under Abbas, had

161

hastened to him, were surprised by Yazid and were compelled to do him homage. Others were won over by gold and became traitors. Nevertheless, with a handful of his loyal subjects, Walid offered a strong resistence to the rebels. But when Abbas also was seen among the rebels, many unsheathed their swords, and no other course was left but to persuade them back to obedience. He reminded the disloyal troops of the high salary granted to them, the landowners of the reduced taxes, and the bulk of the population of their material prosperity. When these words bore no fruit; for the opposition against him had its origin not in any worldly interests but in religious zeal; he suggested a fresh election of the Caliph, but Yazid would not accede to it. Then he withdrew into a room with the words " it is a day not unlike the day of Othman " and read the Qu'ran until the rebels stormed the castle and beheaded him. (16th April 744). On the following day his head was carried about in the streets on the point of a lance, and his own brother Sulaiman, to whom the body was brought for burial, refused to show to it the last honours.

Yazid III could not expect that in a country where the monarchical principles had struck so deep a root, his procedure, despite the contempt in which Walid was held for his light-mindedness and evil ways of living, would meet with general approval. Moreover, it was quite enough that he should have ascended the throne with the help of the Yamanides, to excite the wrath of the descendants of Mudar. This feeling of bitterness was the more heightened and aggravated by the fact that on his mother's side the murdered Caliph belonged to them.

To this was added the fact that Yazid, though severely religious, was nevertheless disliked by the orthodox because of his belief in free-will. The town of Hims at first refused its homage to him, and the mourning women summoned the people to avenge the blood of Walid. But, instead of defending themselves in this well-fortified town and making it the centre of discontent for others equally disaffected, the people of Hims advanced against Damascus and were beaten by the troops of Yazid and were brought back to obedience. A second insurrection in Palestine, headed by Yazid, a son of the Caliph Sulaiman, and his uncle Mohamed, a son of Abdul Malik, was similarly suppressed. In Iraq and Khorasan the Governors of Yazid were not recognized. He had to appoint others to fight the rebels. Specially in Khorasan, a strong, ante-Omayyad party was formed, which later became so powerful that it could neither be controlled nor completely destroyed. Merwan Ibn Mohamed, the Governor of Armenia and Adherbaijan, was the most dangerous enemy of Yazid. This very Merwan had, in vain, warned Yazid against putting himself at the head of rebels. Merwan wrote to Omar, the brother of the murdered Caliph, as soon as he was informed of the occurrences in Damascus, that he was ready to avenge the blood of the Caliph upon the rebels who had broken the oath of loyalty; and shortly after he set out with his army from Caucasus and attacked Mesopotamia, where his son Abdul Malik had taken possession of the town of Harran. Many thousands had voluntarily joined him there. Merwan was already on the point of proceeding against Damascus when Yazid suggested to him a sort of arrangement regarding the division of the Empire. The Caliph wanted not only to confirm him in his Governorship but also desired to make over the whole of Mesopotamia to him. With this offer, very likely, there were other concessions attached, regarding succession and the fate of the imprisioned sons of Walid. But we have no knowledge of them, because Yazid died soon after the homage of Merwan (October 744). As soon as Merwan received information of the death of Yazid, he set out with a powerful army from Harran for Syria, to take over the regency in the name of the sons of Walid, imprisoned in Damascus. In the meantime they had done homage at Damascus to Ibrahim, a brother of Yazid, but he was so weak and worthless that he would not receive homage as Caliph but only as an *Amir*. His brothers who opposed Merwan at Kineserin were defeated and captured. Thence Merwan advanced to Hims, where they had refused to take the oath of allegiance to Ibrahim, but where they received Merwan with open arms. His army, which he now led to Damascus, was re-inforced by a large number of the Mudarites; while the Yamanidas and the hitherto supporters of Yazid flocked round Sulaiman Ibn Hisham, whom Merwan awaited at Ain-ul-Jarr, a small place between Lebanon and Ante-Lebanon, on the way from Balbeck to Damascus. Sulaiman's army was superior to that of Merwan in mere numerical strength, but while, for the most part, they were composed of untrained troops, the army of Merwan consisted of experienced warriors who had taken part in many a campaign in Armenia and Asia Minor. In a murderous battle which remained undecided from early dawn to three in the afternoon, Merwan, by his tactics, at last won the victory. So complete was the defeat of Sulaiman that he had to run away from Damascus with Ibrahim, but before doing so he murdered the sons of Walid and took possession of the treasury. Merwan, who had so far stepped forward only as the avenger of Walid and the protector of his sons, could now boldly advance his claims to the Caliphate. In this course he was strengthened all the more as Abu Mohamed Al Sufyani, a co-prisoner with the sons of Walid, declared that the elder of the two before his death indicated Merwan as his successor to the Caliphate.

In spite of this real or invented sanction, and despite the renunciation by Ibrahim of his claims and the reconciliation of Sulaiman with Merwan—his Government met with opposition on all sides. The subjection of the Yamanides was false and unreal. They remained inwardly hostile to him, and they thirsted for vengeance for the blood which was shed at Ain-ul-Jarr. Wherever it was possible, they rose in rebellion; wherever they were too feeble openly to rise in insurrection they seconded the efforts of the Kharijites and the Hashimites. Merwan's Caliphate was one continuous series of wars against insurrections of all kinds. And yet in spite of his bravery and military capacity and in spite of his unwearied activity and unfailing perseverance which earned for him the surname of *Al-Himar*—he failed to suppress the insurrections which burst forth in all directions. Even the Syrians who had hitherto remained loyal to the Caliphs had now gone over in part to their enemies.

Even in Syria, after few months, unrest showed itself. The leader of the disaffected party was Thabit Ibn Nu'aim, Governor of Palestine, who had sided with the party of Yazid. Hims was stormed and levelled to the ground, and a similar fate overtook the rebellious town of Palmyra; while Mizza, a small town in the neighbourhood of Damascus, the rendezvous of the Yamanides, was given to the flames.

Abdullah Ibn Muawiya, a Hashamite and a descendant of Abu Talib, Mohamed's uncle, rose in Iraq, and when he was forsaken by the Iraqis, as many others had been before him, he, with the help of the Yamanides, took possession of several Persian towns, among others Isphahan, Rayy and Hamadan.

Soon after, Iraq was attacked by the Kharijites, while the Governor deposed by Merwan and the one appointed by him fought with each other in the Province. The Kharijites even became masters of Kufa and Hira. Merwan sent Ibn Hubaira against the Kharijites, but the troops whom he was to lead to Iraq proclaimed Salaiman Ibn Hisham as Caliph, and marched with him to Kinesrin where many other insurgents soon gathered round him.

Merwan was thus forced to relinquish Iraq and to take the field against Sulaiman. In the neighbourhood of Kinesrin he inflicted a bloody defeat upon him, but the beaten troops took quarter at Hims, which was reduced to subjection only after a hard fight (Sept. 746) ; while Sulaiman betook himself to the Kharijites, who were masters of Iraq and the largest portion of Mesopotamia, and later to the Hashimites in Persia.

As soon as Syria was swept clean of the rebels Merwan attacked the Kharijites at Rakka, and compelled them to retire to Mosul. Here they maintained themselves until Ibn Hubaira had taken Kufa and hastened with a portion of his troops to the aid of the Caliph Merwan. (May-June 747). Even in Adher- baijan the Kharijites rose in rebellion, killed the Governor of Merwan, and beat back the troops of the Caliph. The Byzan- tines made inroads into Northern Syria and destroyed the Arab fleet in the neighbourhood of Cyprus. In Mekka the supporters of the Abbasids appeared in black garments and renounced allegiance to Merwan. Medina fell into the hands of the Kharijites, and even in Sanaa the people refused to ack- nowledge the Governor of the Caliph. Thither Merwan was forced to despatch his troops, because he could not let the sacred towns, the meeting-places of the pilgrims, pass into the hands of his enemies. In Africa he had to acknowledge as Governor Abdur Rahman Ibn Habib*, who had driven away Hanzala, the hitherto Omayyad Governor but he left him to himself to fight the Kharijites and the Berbers.

---

* [Abdur Rahman B. Habib, Governor of Ifriqa, died in 137 (755). When his father whom he had in his youth accompanied on raids in Sicily and other places, had fallen in the Berber revolt (142=720), Abdur Rahman fled to Spain but afterwards returned to Africa and rebelled in Tunis in 126 (744) against the Omayyads. The Omayyad Governor Hanzala B. Safwan, thereupon quitted Kairowan, and since the Abbasid uprising was in progress it was not a very difficult task for Abdur Rahman to seize the reins of Government and to keep them. The Abbasids were cunning enough at first

It was an exact description of the Empire which Nasr, the Governor of Khorasan, portrayed in his letter to the Caliph :—

"I see amidst the embers the glow of fire, and it wants but little to burst into a blaze,

And if the wise ones of the people quench it not, its fuel will be corpses and skulls.

Verily fire is kindled by two sticks, and verily words are the beginning of warfare,

And I cry in amazement, 'Would that I knew whether the House of Omayya were awake or asleep."*

Since the accession of Merwan complete anarchy had prevailed in Khorasan, which the emissaries of the Abbasids, working for the last twenty years in that country, managed to turn to their profit. Nasr belonged to the party of the Mudarites, and he therefore caused Al-Kirmani, who stood at the head of the mutinous Yamanides, to be imprisoned. But Al-Kirmani was liberated and had to be fought afresh. Besides him Nasr had to wage war against the rebel Harth, already referred to, who, finding that he could no longer rely upon himself alone, made common cause with Al-Kirmani.

Soon the whole of Khorasan was up in arms. Every one longed for a Government which could restore peace and order, and every one felt that that could not be expected any more from the House of Omayya, divided as it was against itself and resting on no religious and legal foundation.

---

to confirm him in his Governorship. Then when the Caliph Al Mansur threatened to enforce his sovereignty, Abdur Rahman, who was continually making war against Sicily and Sardinia, and the Berbers, renounced all homage to him. Through wishing to settle the succession on his son Habib he incurred the enmity of his two brothers Ilyas and Abdul Warith, who soon afterwards murdered him. Houtsma, Ency. of Islam p. 54 Vol. I. Tr.]

* [See, Browne's Lit. Hist. of Persia Vol. I. p. 241. Tr.]

The Abbasids, taking advantage of the general ill-humour and the inner confusion, publicly asserted (what they had hitherto done only in secret), with the show of force, the rights of the family of the Prophet. Ibrahim, the then head of the family of Abbas, gave the command to the emissary Abu Muslim, mentioned before, to come forward publicly as the defender of the rights of the family of the Prophet to the Caliphate.

As soon as Merwan was informed of this command, Ibrahim had to pay for his ambition with his life, but his two brothers Abdullah Abu-l-Abbas and Abu Jafar luckily escaped to Iraq, where they lived concealed until their party gained the upper hand.

Scarcely had six months elapsed since Abu Muslim had unfurled the black flag of the Abbasids in the little town of Lin, when Nasr found himself compelled to vacate the capital, Merv.

Convinced that the fall of the Omayyads was not very far off, Nasr was on the point of surrendering to Abu Muslim; when he learnt that that course would only mean sure and certain death. Pursued by the troops of Abu Muslim, he withdrew to Nisapur, where he was overtaken and defeated. Yet another defeat he suffered at Jurjan. Pursued by his enemies he thought of finding refuge in Hamadan but on the way death rescued him from further misfortunes (November 748). The remnant of his troops continued their flight to Nehavand. For three months they held the fort there; after which they surrendered to Qahtaba, the Commander-in-Chief of Abu Muslim.

After the capture of Nehavand, the victorious troops marched in two divisions further and further westward across the Tigris and the Euphrates and towards the neighbourhood of Karbala, where Husain had been killed by the Syrians.

There, on that very spot, it was now the turn of the Syrians to suffer a crushing defeat (August 749). Ibn Hubaira, who commanded them, withdrew to Wasit as soon as Kufa had done homage to the Abbasids. Thither also did the Governor of Kufa direct his steps with his loyal troops.

Merwan himself, however, never lost heart. He advanced with his army, which is said to have numbered over 100,000, against the main division of the enemy's army which, during the march of Qahtaba to Karbala, had proceeded across Kurdistan to the river Zab. This army was commanded by Abu Aun, and with it was Abdullah Ibn Ali, an uncle of the first Abbasid Caliph Abdullah Ibn Abbas.

Merwan threw a bridge over the river Zab and hoped to conquer Abu Aun before reinforcements came to his help from Khorasan and Iraq, but many untoward circumstances, notably the treason and ill-will of the Yamanides and the Kharijites who served under him, conspired to rob him of victory. The defeated Syrians took to wild flight, and Merwan, to secure his retreat, was forced to destroy the bridge behind him, and to leave many of his own men exposed to the sword of the enemy. (January 750). Then, indeed, did Merwan try, though in vain, to gather together at Harran a new army to resist Abdullah, who was following closely at his heels.

Failing in his purpose Merwan fled to Damascus, where he was unable to maintain himself. As soon as Abdullah showed himself, an insurrection broke out in his favour. The rebels were victorious. They killed the Governor left behind by Merwan, and on the 22nd April 750 the black flags poured into the capital of the Omayyads in triumph, through the numerous gates of Damascus.

Leaving Damascus Merwan fled across Palestine to Egypt, but he was so closely pursued that he could not organize another expedition. Even in the tranquil valley of the Nile

169

22

insurrection became the order of the day. There also the rebels had to be conquered first, and after them the Abbasids who soon overtook him and gave him battle but the fortune of the day was disastrous for Merwan. Once more did he take to flight, but at last he was killed in a church in Upper Egypt (5th, August).

[*Bibliography.*]

(1) Prolégomènes d' Ibn Khaldoun, 3 vols. Paris|1863—8.

(2) Culturgeschichte des Orients unter den Caliphen by Von Kremer.

(3) Culturgeschichtliche Streifzüge auf den Gebiete des Islams by Von Kremer.

(4) Geschichte der herrschenden Ideen des Islams by Von Kremer.

(5) Die Religiös—politischen oppositionsparteien in alten Islam by Wellhausen.

(6) Die Charidschiten unter den ersten Omayyaden by R. E. Brünnow.

(7) Spanish Islam by Dozy and Stokes.

(8) Poesie und Kunst der Araber in Spanien und Sicilien by Schack.

(9) History of Spain by Burke and Hume. 2nd Edition.

(10) Hartmann, Fünf vorträge über den Islam.

(11) Caussin De Perceval's papers on the Arab Musicians in Journal Asiatique.

Tr.]